HEGEL

Texts and Commentary

OTHER BOOKS BY WALTER KAUFMANN

Nietzsche
Critique of Religion and Philosophy (A252)
From Shakespeare to Existentialism (A213)
The Faith of a Heretic (A336)
Hegel: A Reinterpretation (A528a)

POETRY

Goethe's Faust: A New Translation (A328)
Cain and Other Poems
Twenty German Poets

TRANSLATOR AND EDITOR

The Portable Nietzsche
Existentialism from Dostoevsky to Sartre
Judaism and Christianity: Essays by Leo Baeck
Philosophic Classics: Thales to St. Thomas
Philosophic Classics: Bacon to Kant
Religion from Tolstoy to Camus

HEGEL

TEXTS AND COMMENTARY

Hegel's Preface to His System in a New Translation
with Commentary on Facing Pages, and
"Who Thinks Abstractly?"

Translated and Edited by
WALTER KAUFMANN

ANCHOR BOOKS
DOUBLEDAY & COMPANY, INC.
GARDEN CITY, NEW YORK

All translations in this volume are the author's.

Hegel: Texts and Commentary was originally published by Doubleday & Company, Inc., in 1965, as Chapters VIII and IX of *Hegel: Reinterpretation, Texts, and Commentary.*

Anchor Books edition: 1966

Preface for the Anchor Edition

This volume contains the second part of my *Hegel: Reinterpretation, Texts, and Commentary,* unchanged. This part can be read and studied by itself. The first part, containing the intellectual biography of Hegel and the reinterpretation of his thought, is offered in a companion volume. There the reader will find chapters on "Early Development and Influences: 1770–1800," "The First Seven Essays, 1801–1803," "*The Phenomenology,*" "The Logic," "The System," and "Hegel on History"; also a long chapter entitled "Documentation, or Hegel's Development in Letters and Contemporary Reports," a Chronology, and a detailed bibliography both of Hegel's writings and of the literature about Hegel.

There are two reasons for dividing the book into two volumes. First, it did not seem desirable to reduce the size of the print and crowd the pages to the extent that would have been required to issue the whole of the original volume in one paperback. Far better to have two volumes.

Secondly, some readers may be interested in the intellectual biography and reinterpretation without feeling inclined to make a close study of the preface to *The Phenomenology,* with commentary. Conversely, some professors may wish to read this preface with their students, but not the reinterpretation.

Both volumes can be read independently. There are some cross references; but then there are also references to other works. The index contains references to both volumes. Only references that begin with Roman numerals are to the present volume. The others show the reader where he can find further information on various points.

I am delighted by the reception of the hardcover edition and hope that the Anchor edition may help to revive interest in Hegel.

Contents

PREFACE FOR THE ANCHOR EDITION   ix

The Preface to the *Phenomenology:* Translation with Commentary on Facing Pages   1

Philosophy must become scientific   7
1. Science is not the naked result   7
2. Inner necessity that philosophy become scientific   15
3. External necessity that philosophy become scientific   21

The idea of a phenomenology of the spirit   29
1. The true not only substance but also subject   29
2. What is phenomenology?   41
3. Whose spirit? Individual or universal?   45

Truth   57
1. The forms of consciousness and truth   57
2. Historical and mathematical truths   63
3. Philosophical truth   71

Conclusion   89
1. The exertion of the Concept   89
2. There is no royal road to science   103
3. The philosopher and the public   109

"Who Thinks Abstractly?" (Translation)   113

INDEX   119

ACKNOWLEDGMENTS   131

Abbreviations

The following abbreviations have been used for works cit●
often:

B   *Briefe von und an Hegel,* 4 vols. (1952–60)

C   Commentary on V–PG

D   Chapter VII of the companion volume (Anch●
        Books A528a)

Dok. *Dokumente zu Hegels Entwicklung,* ed. Hoffmeist●
        (1936)

E   Hegel's *Encyclopedia,* 3rd ed. (1830)

EGP   Hegel's *Einleitung in die Geschichte der Philosophi●*
        critical ed. by Hoffmeister (1940)

H   Cross references to *sections* of the companion volum●
        (Anchor Books A528a)

PG   Hegel's *Phänomenologie des Geistes,* ed. Lass●
        (1907)

Ros.   Rosenkranz, *Hegels Leben* (1844)

VG   Hegels' *Die Vernunft in der Geschichte,* critical ●
        by Hoffmeister (1955). All references are ●
        Hegel's own MS unless the page number is f●
        lowed by an "L" to indicate that the citation ●
        based on the students' lecture notes.

V–PG   Hegel's *Vorrede* (Preface) to the *Phänomenologie*

WK   Kaufmann, *From Shakespeare to Existentialism* (A●
        chor ed.)

HEGEL

Texts and Commentary

The Preface to the *Phenomenology*:
Translation with Commentary on Facing Pages

. . . it is not saying too much when I claim that anyone
understands Hegel's philosophy if he completely masters
the meaning of this preface.

RUDOLF HAYM, *Hegel und seine Zeit* (1857), 215.

. . . the most important of all Hegel texts . . . Whoever
has understood the preface to the *Phenomenology* has
understood Hegel.

HERMANN GLOCKNER, *Hegel,* vol. II (1940), xx, 419.

The Preface to the *Phenomenology* is one of the greatest
philosophical undertakings of all times. . . . HERBERT
MARCUSE, *Reason and Revolution: Hegel and the Rise of
Social Theory* (1941), 97.

The *Phenomenology* is preceded by a remarkable *Preface,* which is a literary as well as a philosophical masterpiece. 		J. N. FINDLAY, *Hegel* (1958), 83.

The preface roars like a romantic symphony . . . I compare it to a world-historical festival. . . .

GUSTAV EMIL MÜLLER, *Hegel* (1959), 203.

he original text of Hegel's long preface is far from easy to
nderstand. This fact poses problems for the translator which
re alleviated but not solved by the addition of a commentary
n facing pages. In all of my other translations, including
nose in the present volume, I have aimed at the greatest
ossible faithfulness, to the point of giving the reader some

feeling for the author's style. The following translation tak
greater liberties than I am wont to take, but is still faithful.

Where the meaning is in doubt, or two interpretations a
possible, I have not considered it my task to make up Hegel
mind. Where he is ambiguous, I have tried to be. I have n
knowingly changed his meaning.

As far as possible, his tone is preserved, too. The alternati
between cumbersome sentences that go on much too lo
and powerful epigrams that spell temporary relief is one
the most striking characteristics of this preface. But for t
most part Hegel's excessively long sentences had to be brok
up a little. He relies heavily on pronouns, both personal ar
relative, and in German the gender usually makes clear
what they refer, even if the referent is found many lines bac
In English, lacking the guide of gender, one often has to repe
the referent—and one frequently has to begin a new sentenc
Moreover, Hegel begins many sentences with such locutio
as "For how and what it would be suitable to say. . . ." O
"Also because. . . ." Or: "As firm as. . . ."; "At the sar
time, when. . . ."; "Just as much. . . ."

That all this is exceedingly awkward, there is no denyin
but in German it is not as unusual as it would be in Englis
It may be one of the lesser values of the many quotatio
from other writers in this volume that they remind us ho
awkwardly ever so many Germans wrote during this perio
—or *at least* during this period.

In sum: the translation is, I believe, easier to follow tha
the original. Occasionally, splendid lines have been liberate
from the coils of incredibly long sentences. Moreover, Hege
long paragraphs have been broken up; and this device, to
allows one to call a little more attention to some sentences I
letting them conclude a paragraph.

In this connection, Hegel's letter to Hinrichs, April 7, 182
is relevant: "Even this would make things easier if you ma
more notches in your paragraphs and broke them up in
more sections: the five first pages are one paragraph; the s
following ones, ditto; etc." Hegel's paragraphs had nev
been as long as those of his young disciple; and by 1821 Heg
had developed a manner of writing *very* short paragraphs,

ompendium style. I have aimed at striking a reasonable
medium.

Hegel's all too abundant italics are more confusing than
helpful. In the *Phenomenology,* German editors do not re-
roduce them, nor do I.

In the commentary I have inserted relatively few references
to my reinterpretation. Naturally, I believe that a reading of
the complete reinterpretation would be a great help in understanding the text. Chapter III, which deals with *The Phenome-
ology of the Spirit,* is obviously most relevant, and even a
glance at the table of contents will give some idea of the topics
treats. I should like to call special attention to section 34,
on "Hegel's terminology."

Hegel's characteristic terms are by no means always his
coinages. *Weltgeist* (world spirit), for example, had been
used by Kant, Herder, and Mendelssohn before him, and is
also encountered in Schelling's and Schopenhauer's works.
Some other terms now widely associated with Hegel were
introduced by Schiller in his essay "On the Aesthetic Education of Man" (H 7). *An und für sich* (in and for itself), *an
sich* (in itself), and *für uns* (for us) occur together on page
7 of Fichte's *Sun-clear Report* (1801), and in the same book
Fichte contrasts, in passing, *räsonnieren* (argumentative
thinking) and philosophizing. It would be as silly to say that
Hegel stole these terms from others as it would be to suppose
that he made them up as he went along, in a deliberate effort
to be quaint: the point is rather that much that may seem
strange today was not so far-fetched at the time. Hegel used
expressions that were then current and, as often as not, gave
them a new twist.

In an aphorism of the Berlin period, Hegel said: "a great
man condemns men to explicate him" (Ros. 555). For a com-
mentator this is an appropriate motto, but Hegel was almost
certainly not thinking of himself, and the motto is as apt for
this preface as it is for my commentary: we are all condemned,
as Hegel sees it, to try to comprehend what man has thought
up to our time and to relive, in condensed form, the experiences of the world spirit. The preface that follows is of a
piece with the conclusion of Hegel's introductory lectures on

the philosophy of history: "The moments which the spirit
seems to have left behind, it also possesses in its present depth.
As it has run through its moments in history, it has to run
through them in the present—in the Concept of itself" (VG
183 L).

The parallel to Freud should not be missed. Indeed, the
first of these two sentences might well have been written by
Freud, except that he would probably have said "soul," not
"spirit." But the second sentence, too, is reminiscent of psychoanalysis: recapitulating our past is the price of freedom.

* * *

Hegel's own description of the *Phenomenology* appeared in
the Jena cultural supplement not before publication, as was
then customary for *Selbstanzeigen*,[1] but on October 28, 1807.

"Announcements of new books:

"Jos. Ant. Goebhardt's Bookstore, Bamberg and Würzburg,
has published and sent to all good bookstores: G. W. F.
Hegel's *System of Science*. Volume One, containing *The Phenomenology of the Spirit*. Large Octavo. 1807. Price: 6 fl.

"This volume deals with the *becoming of knowledge*. The
phenomenology of the spirit is to replace psychological explanations as well as the more abstract discussions of the
foundation of knowledge. It considers the *preparation* for science from a point of view, which makes it a new, an interesting, and the first science of philosophy. It includes the various
forms of the spirit as stations on the way on which it becomes
pure knowledge or absolute spirit. In the main parts of this
science, which in turn are subdivided further, consideration
is given to consciousness, self-consciousness, observing and
acting reason, the spirit itself as ethical, educated, and moral
spirit, and finally as religious in its different forms. The wealth
of the appearances of the spirit, which at first glance seem
chaotic, is brought into a scientific order which presents them
according to their necessity in which the imperfect ones dissolve and pass over into higher ones which constitute their

[1] The author's description of his book.

next truth. Their final truth they find at first in religion, then in science as the result of the whole.

"In the preface the author explains himself about what seems to him the need of philosophy in its present state; also about the presumption and mischief of the philosophic formulas that are currently degrading philosophy, and about what is altogether crucial in it and its study.

"A *second volume* will contain the system of *Logic* as speculative philosophy, and of the other two parts of philosophy, the *sciences* of *nature* and the *spirit*."

Hegel's own Table of Contents (1807)[2]

1 Of scientific knowledge

2 The element of truth is the Concept, and its true form the scientific system

3 Present position of the spirit

4 The principle is not the completion; against formalism

5 The absolute is subject—

6 —and what this is

7 The element of knowledge

8 The ascent into this is the Phenomenology of the Spirit

9 The transmutation of the notion and the familiar into thought—

10 —and this into the Concept

11 In what way the Phenomenology of the Spirit is negative or contains what is false

12 Historical and mathematical truth

13 The nature of philosophical truth and its method

14 Against schematizing formalism

15 The demands of the study of philosophy

16 Argumentative thinking in its negative attitude—

17 —in its positive attitude; its subject

18 Natural philosophizing as healthy common sense and as genius

19 Conclusion: the author's relation to the public

[2] Only the part covering the preface has been translated here. In the original the headings are run on and not numbered.

TRANSLATION

1. Of scientific knowledge[1]

[I.1]

In the preface of a book it is customary to explain the au
thor's aim, the reasons why he wrote the book, and what h
takes to be its relationship to other treatments, earlier or con
temporary, of the same subject. In the case of a philosophica
work, however, such an explanation seems not only superfluou
but, owing to the nature of the subject matter,[2] altogether in
proper and unsuited to the end in view. For what contents an
tone would be appropriate for a preface to a philosophica
work? Perhaps a historical statement concerning the tendenc
and point of view, the general contents and results of the work
an attempt to connect sundry claims and assertions about th
truth? Philosophical truth cannot be presented in this manne

Philosophy deals essentially with the general in which th
particular is subsumed. Therefore it *seems,* more than in th
case of other sciences, as if the aim or the final results gav
expression to the subject matter itself, even as if they did entir
justice to its very essence, while the way in which things ar
worked out in detail may seem to be unessential. Yet peopl
do not suppose that the general idea of, say, the nature o
anatomy—perhaps as the knowledge of the parts of the bod
considered *qua* their lifeless existence—automatically furnishe
us with the subject matter itself. Everybody realizes that, if w
want possession of the contents of this science, we must als
exert ourselves to master the particulars, the detail.

Moreover, such an aggregate of information really has n
right to the name of science; and any discussion of its aim an
other such generalities is usually no different from the manne
in which the content—i.e., the nerves, the muscles, etc.—is di
cussed, too: in both cases, the manner is equally historica
and void of Concepts.[3] In the case of philosophy, howeve
such an introductory discussion would be an oddity: for

COMMENTARY

I. *Philosophy must become scientific*

1. Science is not the naked result

¹ In the first edition of 1807, the table of contents includes nineteen subheads under the preface. They are not numbered as in our text but run on, interrupted only by Roman numeral page numbers. In the text itself no divisions are indicated. These headings afford some insight into Hegel's intentions and are worth reproducing. In the text they are numbered consecutively and italicized. In Hegel's table of contents, the first heading is not assigned a page number but immediately followed by the second; yet it surely belongs at the outset.

In the first critical edition of the work (1907), the editor, Georg Lasson, divided the preface into four major parts, and each of these into three sections. In his text these are indicated respectively by Roman and Arabic numerals, and in his table of contents, which does not follow the original one at this point, these four Roman and twelve Arabic numbers are followed by titles he proposed. His disposition is plausible and helpful and therefore reproduced in the commentary, but our titles (in *italics*) and subtitles (in Roman letters) are not his. In sum, Hegel's own subheads appear in the texts, ours in the commentary, opposite the places (marked by numerals only) where they belong.

² "Subject matter": in German, *Sache*. This word can mean: thing, matter, concern. *Zur Sache!* can mean: to the subject; and *das gehört nicht zur Sache:* that is irrelevant. *Sachlich* can also mean: objective; and *bei der Sache sein:* to concentrate.

³ "historical and void of Concepts": in German, *historisch und begrifflos*. The only previous translation, Baillie's (1910, revised 1931; reprinted also in Scribner's *Hegel Selections*) has: "descriptive and superficial." Plainly, this is not what Hegel says. The ordinary meaning of *Begriff* is definitely

would employ this same manner while demonstrating that this manner is incapable of grasping the truth.[4]

The very attempt to determine the relationship of a philosophical work to other efforts concerning the same subject, introduces an alien and irrelevant interest which obscures precisely that which matters for the recognition of the truth. Opinion considers the opposition of what is true and false quite rigid, and, confronted with a philosophical system, it expects agreement or contradiction. And in an explanation of such a system, opinion still expects to find one or the other. It does not comprehend the difference of the philosophical systems in terms of the progressive development of the truth, but sees only the contradiction in this difference. The bud disappears as the blossom bursts forth, and one could say that the former is refuted by the latter. In the same way, the fruit declares the blossom to be a false existence of the plant, and the fruit supplants the blossom as the truth of the plant. These forms do not only differ, they also displace each other because they are incompatible. Their fluid[5] nature, however, makes them, at the same time, elements of an organic unity in which they not only do not conflict, but in which one is as necessary as the other; and it is only this equal necessity that constitutes the life of the whole.[6]

The opposition to a philosophical system, however, usually does not understand itself in this way. And the consciousness that is confronted with this opposition usually does not know how to liberate it, or how to keep it free, from its one-sidedness. Nor does it know how to penetrate this appearance of contention and mutual opposition in order to recognize elements which are necessary to each other.

The demand for such explanations or confessions and the satisfaction of this demand are easily mistaken for a concern with what is essential. Where could one hope for a better expression of the core of a philosophical work than in its aims and results? And how could these be determined better than by noting their difference from that which the age generally produces in the same sphere? But when this procedure is taken for more than the beginning of knowledge, when it is mistaken for knowledge itself, then we must indeed count it among the

concept. Because this is one of Hegel's most characteristic terms, and he associates more than its ordinary meaning with it, some nineteenth-century English translators felt that a less ordinary term was called for and hit on "notion." This word is utterly misleading as it suggests vagueness and caprice, while Hegel takes pains to *attack* haziness and subjectivity, opposing to them "the seriousness of the Concept" (cf. [11] below). He upholds rigorous and highly disciplined conceptual analysis. *Begriff* is closely related to *begreifen* (to comprehend)—an affinity that unfortunately cannot be recaptured in English—and Hegel considers it the task of philosophy to comprehend and not merely to feel and rhapsodize.

[4] The oddity here noted is indeed a striking characteristic of the preface that follows. (Cf. H 14, 24 f., and 37.)

[5] "fluid": this image is picked up again later in the preface: see II.3, note [35] below.

[6] This is one of the most interesting and fateful paragraphs in Hegel's writings. In Descartes, Hobbes, and Spinoza, in Locke, Berkeley, and Hume, or in Kant we find no comparable conception of philosophical disagreement or "the progressive development of the truth." Different philosophies, according to Hegel, are not to be viewed as laid out next to each other in a spatial arrangement; they cannot be fully understood as long as their temporal relationship is ignored. Studying a single system is like studying, say, a blossom; the study of the whole plant and of living organisms corresponds to the study of the development of philosophy to the present time. Different philosophies represent different stages of maturity.

Here, then, at the beginning of his first book, Hegel announces the vision that led him about fifteen years later, as a professor at the University of Berlin, to establish the history of philosophy as a subject of central importance for students of philosophy—which it had not been before. (But see H 67, n. [40].)

"Necessary" and "necessity" in the last sentence are questionable. Hegel means that philosophies should not be understood as capricious webs spun by wayward thinkers but as significant stages in the development of thought. When a philosopher disagrees with his predecessors, we should not reject the lot because they cannot agree with each other; rather we should ask how the later thinkers correct the partiality of the former, and how each contributes to the gradual refinement

devices for by-passing the real subject matter, while combining the semblance of seriousness and exertion with a dispensation from both.

For the subject matter is not exhausted by any aim, but only by the way in which things are worked out in detail; nor is the result the actual whole, but only the result together with its becoming. The aim, taken by itself, is a lifeless generality; the tendency is a mere drift which still lacks actuality; and the naked result is the corpse which has left the tendency behind.[7]

In the same way, the difference is really the limit of the subject matter: it indicates where the subject matter ceases, or it is what the subject matter is not. Such exertions concerning the aim, the results, the differences that may exist in this respect, or the critical judgments of aim and results, are therefore easier work than they may seem to be. For instead of dealing with the subject matter, such talk is always outside it; instead of abiding in the subject matter and forgetting itself in it, such knowledge always reaches out for something else and really remains preoccupied with itself instead of sticking to, and devoting itself to, the subject matter.[8]

To judge that which has contents and workmanship is the easiest thing; to grasp it is more difficult; and what is most difficult is to combine both by producing an account of it.[9]

How should education begin, and how the process of working oneself up out of the immediacy of the substance of life? The beginning will always have to be made by acquiring some cognizance of general principles and points of view and by working oneself up, first of all, to the idea[10] of the subject matter. No less, one must learn to support or refute it with reasons, to comprehend a concrete and copious fullness in terms of exact determinations, and to be able to offer accurate information and serious judgments. Then, however, this beginning of education will have to give way to the seriousness of life in its fullness which leads us into the experience of the subject matter itself. And when, in addition to all this, the seriousness of the Concept[11] descends into the depth of the subject matter, then such knowledge and judgment will always retain a proper place in discussion.

of knowledge. Hegel notwithstanding, this does not imply any genuine necessity. Hegel often uses "necessary" quite illicitly as the negation of "utterly arbitrary."

[7] Most English-speaking philosophers 150 years after this was written would agree with this paragraph. A student who remembers and reproduces the conclusions of his teacher, or of some great philosopher, but not the way in which things are worked out in detail, has only got hold of something lifeless: the spirit of philosophy has escaped him. What counts in philosophy is not the striking aim or claim, but the detail.

[8] What is wanted is devotion. The philosopher, like a scientist, should devote himself to, and immerse himself in, his subject instead of trying to be interesting and different. Or as Hegel puts it later, what is wanted is "the seriousness of the Concept."

[9] External criticism that simply condemns without any prior effort to comprehend is relatively easy and trivial. To really grasp a position and the arguments involved in it is more difficult. But a philosopher must combine grasp and critical evaluation: for until we rethink every step critically we cannot fully comprehend what led a writer to go on as he did; what problems led him to develop his views; and what prompted later thinkers to differ with him.

[10] "idea": German, *Gedanke;* literally, "thought." Translated as "idea" at this point because this is more idiomatic here.

[11] "the seriousness of the Concept": *der Ernst des Begriffs* is one of Hegel's famous phrases. For *Begriff* see note [3] above. This term is rendered, throughout this translation, as Concept—with a capital C to signal that Hegel uses this word as a technical term. Here, for example, "the seriousness of conceptual analysis" would be a little more idiomatic.

Some of the preceding might strike readers with no predilection for philosophy as an invitation to pedantry. But consider the Philistine who reads the final speech of Goethe's *Faust,* in the fifth act of Part Two, and says: "I always knew that nothing good could come of boundless striving; one has to settle down to a job and do it well." He has got hold of a "naked result" or a "lifeless generality." Real comprehension depends on a grasp neither of the play without the last act, nor of the speech without the play, but of "the result together with its becoming." (Cf. Hegel's Jena aphorism #45 in *Dok.*) In the case of a philosophic position, too, the "becoming" in-

2. The element of truth is the Concept, and its true form the scientific system[12]

The true form in which truth exists can only be the scientific system of it. To contribute to this end, that philosophy might come closer to the form of science—the goal being that it might be able to relinquish the name of love of knowledge and be actual knowledge—that is what I have resolved to try. The *inner* necessity according to which knowledge is science is grounded in the nature of knowledge, and the only satisfactory explanation of this is to be found in the presentation of philosophy itself. The *external* necessity, however, can also be understood more generally, apart from the accidents of the author's person or his individual motivation; and so understood, it coincides with the inner necessity; only the form is different in accordance with the manner in which time exhibits the existence of its stages. To demonstrate that the time has come for the elevation of philosophy to a science[13]—this would be the only true justification of the attempts which have this aim. For this would show the necessity of this aim even while accomplishing it.

volves not only the detailed arguments but also "the seriousness of life in its fullness" (*Ernst des erfüllten Lebens*). Yet
this, however necessary, is not enough for philosophy which
requires, "in addition to all this, the seriousness of the Concept."

[12] The page number assigned to this heading in the original edition (vii) is clearly mistaken (vi must be meant); vii
would move it down one paragraph.

[13] Fichte already had spoken of his "exertions to elevate
philosophy to a science," on the second page of his preface
to *Sun-clear Report to the Public at Large about the True
Nature of the Newest Philosophy: An attempt to compel the
readers to understand* (Berlin, 1801). "The time has come
for": *an der Zeit ist;* a common idiomatic expression that is
ill rendered by Baillie's "the time process does raise philosophy . . ."

[I.2]

Truth can attain its true form only by becoming scientific, or, in other words, I claim that truth finds the element of its existence only in the Concept. I know that this view seems to contradict a notion[1] and its consequences that are as presumptuous as they are widely accepted in our time. Therefore some discussion of this contradiction seems hardly superfluous, although at this point it can only take the form of a mere assertion—just like the view against which it is aimed.

Others say that truth exists only in that, or rather as that, which is called now intuition,[2] now immediate knowledge of the absolute, religion, or being—not *at* the center of divine love but the being itself of this very center.[3] It follows that what is then demanded for the presentation of philosophy is the opposite of the form of the Concept. The absolute is supposed to be not comprehended[4] but felt and intuited; it is not its Concept that is meant to prevail and be proclaimed but its feeling and intuition.

3. Present position of the spirit

The appearance of such a demand should be considered in its more general context, and one should see what stage the self-conscious spirit occupies at present. Clearly, it has passed beyond the substantial life that it formerly led in the element of thought—beyond this immediacy of its faith, beyond the satisfaction and security of that certainty which consciousness possessed about its reconciliation with the essence and its general, internal as well as external, presence. The spirit has not only passed beyond all this into the other extreme of its insubstantial reflection in itself; it has also passed beyond that. Not only has it lost its essential life; it is also conscious of this loss and of the finitude that is its contents. The spirit is turning away from the husks[5] and, confessing that it is in trouble and cursing, it now demands from philosophy not so much self-knowledge as that philosophy should help the spirit to establish such substantiality and the solidity of being. Philosophy is

I.2. Inner necessity that philosophy become scientific

In keeping with the preceding paragraph, Hegel proceeds to discuss, first, the "inner necessity" and then (I.3) the "external necessity."

¹ "notion": *Vorstellung*. This German word is usually rendered, by translators of Kant and Schopenhauer, as either "representation" or "idea." The former is literally correct but often, as in the present context, exceedingly clumsy. "Idea," on the other hand, is often needed to render the German *Idee*. An examination of all occurrences of *Vorstellung* in this long preface shows that Hegel generally means to suggest something vague and distinctly less scientific than a Concept. "Notion" seems just right.

² "intuition": *Anschauung*. This translation seems firmly established in English translations of German philosophy; and according to the *Shorter Oxford English Dictionary*, "intuition" means in "*Mod. Philos.* the immediate apprehension of an object by the mind without the intervention of any reasoning process." This sense, which goes back to 1600, is exactly right here.

³ Mid-twentieth-century readers may associate this view with Paul Tillich, without realizing that Tillich wrote his doctoral dissertation on Schelling and owes much to German romanticism. Lasson, in 1907, associated the views criticized here with "Jacobi, the romantics, Schlegel, and Schleiermacher."

⁴ "comprehended": *begriffen*. "Concept": *Begriff*.

⁵ "husks" (*Treber*) alludes to the parable of the prodigal son, Luke 15:16. Cf. Schiller, *On the Aesthetic Education of Man, in a Series of Letters* (1795): "Nature (sense) unifies everywhere, the understanding differentiates everywhere, but reason unifies again. Hence man, before he begins to philosophize, is closer to the truth than the philosopher who has not yet concluded his inquiry" (note to the 18th Letter). Hegel scorns those who, at the first differentiation when they find they are far from home, turn back instead of persevering, pushing on the inquiry, and comprehending the truth. In his opposition to *Schwärmerei*, the cult of feeling, and the inspirational philosophizing of the pious, Hegel does not pit reason against passion, or academic pedantry against deep experi-

asked to answer this need not by unlocking the locks of substance and raising it to the level of self-consciousness, nor by returning the chaotic consciousness to the order of thought and the simplicity of the Concept, but rather by confounding the distinctions of thought, by suppressing the discriminating Concept, and by establishing the *feeling* of the essence,[6] granting not so much insight as edification.

The beautiful, the holy, the eternal, religion, and love are the bait that is required to arouse the desire to bite. Not the Concept but ecstasy, not the coldly progressing necessity of the subject matter but fermenting enthusiasm is held to be the best attitude and guide to the spread-out riches of the substance.[7]

In line with such demands one exerts oneself almost zealously and angrily to tear men out of their absorption in the sensuous, the vulgar, the particular, and to raise their sights to the stars—as if, utterly forgetful of the divine, they were at the point of satisfying themselves with dust and water, like worms. Formerly they had a heaven, furnished with abundant riches of thoughts and images. The significance of all that is used to lie in the thread of light that tied it to the heavens; and following this thread, the eye, instead of abiding in the present, rose above that to the divine essence, to, if one may say so, a presence beyond. The eye of the spirit had to be directed forcibly to the things of this earth and kept there. Indeed, it took a long time to work that clarity which only the supernatural possessed into the must and confusion in which the sense[8] of this world lay imprisoned; it took a long time to make attention to the present as such—what was called, in one word, experience—interesting and valid.

Now the opposite need meets the eye: sense[8] seems to be so firmly rooted in what is worldly that it takes an equal force to raise it higher. The spirit appears so poor that, like a wanderer in the desert who languishes for a simple drink of water, it seems to crave for its refreshment merely the bare feeling of the divine in general. By that which suffices the spirit one can measure the extent of its loss.

This modest contentment in accepting, or stinginess in giving, is, however, improper for science. Whoever seeks mere

nce; instead he questions the seriousness of th
he depth of the experience of the writers he
un back home as soon as the going gets rough
ack of strength in a mist of emotion.

[6] "the *feeling* of the essence": *das Gefüh*
Baillie: "the feeling of existence."

[7] It is the beauty of Hegel's criticisms tha
ected against some of his contemporaries, they
pplicable to many well-known writers in other

[8] "sense": the German in both places is *Si*
He has "sense" the first time and "mind and inter
nd, thus missing some of the contrast.

Hegel juxtaposes the otherworldliness of the p
orldliness of the present.

Lasson has a note at the point where our [7] appears. This
description of the spiritual situation of the age corresponds to
he section on the 'unhappy consciousness,' " later in the book.
But the immediately preceding sentence (split into two sen-
ences in our translation) does not necessarily imply any otherworldliness: it might be applied, for example, to Jaspers and
Tillich. Only the passage beginning "Formerly they had . . ."
invites comparison with the "unhappy consciousness" (see
I 33). On the whole, Lasson is a very helpful guide.

edification, whoever desires to shroud the worldly multiplicit
of his existence and of thought in a fog to attain the indeter
minate enjoyment of this indeterminate divinity, may look ou
for himself where he can find this; he will easily find the mean
to impress himself with his enthusiasm and thus to puff himsel
up. Philosophy, however, must beware of wishing to b
edifying.[9]

Least of all should such modest contentment which re
nounces science make claims that such ecstasy and dimnes
are something higher than science. Such prophetic talk sup
poses that it abides right in the center and in the depths, view:
the determinate (*the horos*) contemptuously,[10] and deliber
ately keeps its distance from the Concept and from necessity
associating them with reflection[11] that makes its home in th
finite. But even as there is an empty breadth, there is also a
empty depth; even as there is an extension of the substanc
that pours itself out into finite multiplicity without the strengt
to hold it together, there is also an intensity void of content-
pure force without any spread—which is identical with super
ficiality. The strength of the spirit is only as great as its ex
pression; its depth is only as deep as it dares to spread an
lose itself in its explication.[12]

Moreover, when this substantial knowledge without Con
cept[13] pretends to have drowned the personality of the self i
the essence and to philosophize in a true and holy manner, i
really hides the truth from itself: for instead of devoting itsel
to the god, it is undone because it spurns measure and deter
mination, and now the accidental contents, now persona
arbitrariness will lord it.—As they abandon themselves to th
untamed ferment of the substance,[14] they suppose that b
shrouding self-consciousness and yielding up the understandin
they become His beloved to whom God gives wisdom i
sleep;[15] what they thus conceive and give birth to in slee
indeed are, naturally, dreams.

⁹ Hegel's polemic against mere "edification" and the wish to be "edifying" (*erbaulich*) brings to mind Kierkegaard's *Edifying Discourses*. Kierkegaard's many polemical references to Hegel are better known than the fact that Hegel published his critique of Kierkegaard six years before the latter was born. Kierkegaard's authorship of *Edifying Discourses* and *Concluding Unscientific Postscript* has to be understood against the background not only of Hegel's *Logic*, which is usually cited in this connection, but also of the *Phenomenology*, which is too often ignored by Kierkegaard's expositors.

¹⁰ Hegel here sides with Plato against those who despise the limit and the determinate instead of realizing that this is the element of reason. Like Plato, he is aware of the power of poetry and passion, but considers the definite and precise superior to the indefinite and amorphous.

¹¹ "reflection": *Reflexion*. The German and English words have the same double meaning.

¹² "empty depth": a splendid phrase, by no means applicable only to the romantics of whom Hegel was thinking primarily. The last sentence offers a superb formulation of one of Sartre's central ideas: "for the existentialist, there is no love apart from the deeds of love; . . . there is no genius other than that which is expressed in works of art. The genius of Proust is the totality of the works of Proust . . . In life, a man . . . draws his own portrait and there is nothing but that portrait. . . . 'You are nothing else but what you live.'" "Existentialism is a Humanism" in *Existentialism from Dostoevsky to Sartre*, ed. Walter Kaufmann, 300 f.

¹³ "this substantial knowledge without Concept": *dies begrifflose substantielle Wissen*. Baillie: "this unreflective emotional knowledge."

¹⁴ "of the substance": *der Substanz*. Baillie: "of sheer emotion."

¹⁵ An allusion to Psalms 127:2, which is often cited in German.

[I.3]

It is surely not difficult to see that our time is a time of birt
and transition to a new period. The spirit has broken with wha
was hitherto the world of its existence and imagination and i
about to[1] submerge all this in the past; it is at work givin
itself a new form. To be sure, the spirit is never at rest bu
always engaged in[2] ever progressing motion. But just as in th
case of a child the first breath it draws after long silent nour
ishment terminates the gradualness of the merely quantitativ
progression—a qualitative leap[3]—and now the child is born, s
too, the spirit that educates itself[4] matures slowly and quietl
toward the new form, dissolving one particle of the edifice c
its previous world after the other, while its tottering is sug
gested only by some symptoms here and there: frivolity a
well as the boredom that open up in the establishment and th
indeterminate apprehension of something unknown are har
bingers of a forthcoming change. This gradual crumblin
which did not alter the physiognomy of the whole is inter
rupted by the break of day that, like lightning, all at once re
veals the edifice of the new world.[5]

Yet what is new here does not have perfect actuality an
more than the newborn child; and it is essential not to over
look this.[6] The first emergence is only its immediacy or it
Concept.[7] Even as a building is not finished when its founda

I.3. External necessity that philosophy become scientific

[1] "imagination": *Vorstellens;* literally, representing. "is about to": *steht im Begriff;* a common idiom that means, is about to. Baillie: "is in the mind to."

[2] "engaged in": *ist . . . begriffen;* another idiom. At first glance, the relation of these two idioms to *Begriff* (Concept) seems quite fortuitous and void of any significance; but Hegel, like Plato and Aristotle, paid attention to such matters and probably found in these expressions some intimation at the level of ordinary language of his own conviction that the Concept is essentially dynamic.

[3] "qualitative leap" has often been quoted from Hegel, and some Marxists have harped on the idea that great quantitative differences eventually become qualitative differences.

[4] "the spirit that educates itself" or "that forms itself": *der sich bildende Geist. Bild* means picture or image; *bilden,* to shape or form, but also to educate. *Sich bilden,* the reflexive form, usually means to educate oneself; and *Bildung,* for which there is no entirely adequate translation, education. *Ungebildet* means uneducated, uncultured, uncouth, raw. *Bildungsroman* is the novel that relates the education of the hero; and ever since Goethe published *Wilhelm Meisters Lehrjahre* (1795/96) this genre has attracted many of the best German writers. In his *Lectures on Modern Idealism* (published posthumously in 1919), Royce considered it pretty well extinct (p. 140), but since then Thomas Mann and Hermann Hesse have returned to it again and again. The *Phenomenology of the Spirit* is the story of the *Bildung* of the spirit.

[5] Throughout this paragraph Hegel alludes to the French Revolution; for example, "time of birth and transition," "frivolity" and "boredom," and the "gradual crumbling" that precedes a sudden break.

[6] It is also essential to translate *Wirklichkeit* and *wirklich* as actuality and actual, not as reality and real. The baby is real enough, but if we think in terms of the contrast of potentiality and actuality we can say that "the newborn child" lacks "perfect actuality." Hegel's notorious equation of the actual and the rational is not a sanctification of the *status quo;* in his terminology, most states are not fully actual and rational.

[7] "immediacy" (*Unmittelbarkeit*) means for Hegel quite literally that which has not been mediated or gone through an

tion has been laid, the attained Concept of the whole is no
the whole itself. When we wish to see an oak—the strength o
its trunk, the spread of its branches, and the mass of its foliag
—we are not satisfied when in its place we are shown an acorr
Thus science, the crown[8] of a world of the spirit, is not com
plete in its beginning. The beginning of the new spirit is th
product of a far-reaching revolution in ever so many form
of culture and education;[9] it is the prize for an immensel
tangled path and an equally immense amount of exertion an
toil. It is the whole which has returned into itself from succes
sion as well as extension,[10] the resultant simple Concept of it
But the actuality of this simple whole consists in this, tha
these forms which have become mere moments[11] now develo
anew and give themselves form, but in their new element,[
in the sense that has emerged.

4. The principle is not the completion; against formalism

While on the one hand the first appearance of the ne
world is only the whole shrouded in simplicity or its genera
basis, the wealth of its previous existence is, on the other hand
still present to consciousness in memory.[13] In the newly ap
pearing form it misses the spread and the particularization o
the contents; but even more it misses the cultivation[14] of th
form whereby the distinctions are determined with certaint
and ordered according to their firm relationships. Withou
this elaboration[14] science lacks universal intelligibility[15] an
has the appearance of being an esoteric possession of a fev
individuals. An esoteric possession: for it is present only in it
Concept—only its inside is there. Of a few individuals: for it
inarticulate appearance makes its existence merely individua
Only what is completely determinate is at the same time exo
teric, comprehensible, and capable of being learned and o
thus becoming the property of all. The intelligible[15] form o
science is the way to science which is offered to all and mad
equal for all; and to reach rational knowledge by means o
the understanding[15] is the just demand of consciousness as i
approaches science. For the understanding[15] is thinking, th
pure ego; and the sensible[15] is the already familiar and tha
which science and the unscientific consciousness have in com

ntermediate condition. Babies and acorns, of course, are the results of prior developments, but here they are not considered as results but as what is given in the beginning. When the concept is attained that all men are free, equal, and brothers, a long development may still be required before liberty, equality, and fraternity are fully actualized. (Cf. H 44 and 9 f.)

⁸ In German the top of a tree is often called its crown.

⁹ "revolution in ever so many forms of culture and education": *Umwälzung von mannigfaltigen Bildungsformen.*

¹⁰ The "new spirit" is the product of a long Odyssey of the spirit or, more prosaically, of a journey through time and space, "succession as well as extension."

¹¹ "moments": *Momente.* Hegel frequently uses this term, and his primary meaning is rarely, if ever, instants. The *Shorter Oxford English Dictionary* defines: "One of the elements of a complex conceptual entity. (After Ger. use.) 1863"; and the supporting quotation speaks of "elements or moments." But there is a slight temporal connotation, reflected in one of the other definitions: "A definite stage or turning-point in a course of events 1666." Sometimes "stages" comes a little closer to Hegel's meaning than "elements" would.

¹² The "new element" is philosophy. What has developed must now be comprehended and developed all over again, in thought.

¹³ The partisans of "immediate knowledge" suffer from amnesia: what they claim to know immediately was in fact mediated by a long historical process. What seems self-evident now was not obvious in the past, and what seems simple is in fact the whole development "shrouded in simplicity." (Cf. H 44.)

¹⁴ *Ausbildung.*

¹⁵ "intelligibility": *Verständlichkeit;* "intelligible": *verständlich;* "understanding": *Verstand;* "the sensible": *das Verständige.*

The basic idea of section I.3 so far, and of this paragraph especially, is that the time has come for all men to demand equal access to philosophy; and to become common property philosophy must become scientific. To become exoteric and democratic, philosophy must be available to every intelligent person who is willing to shirk no effort—regardless of whether he belongs to some special group or clique, whether that be

mon—that whereby the latter can immediately enter science

The science which is still close to its beginnings and thu
has achieved neither completeness of detail nor perfection o
form is open to reproach for this reason. But if such censur
is aimed at the very essence of science it is as unjust as i
would be to refuse to recognize the demand for such elabora
tion. This opposition seems to be the most important knot o
which scientific education is working today, wearying itsel
without as yet properly understanding the situation. One sid
insists on the wealth of its material and its intelligibility; th
other side spurns at least the latter and insists on immediat
rationality and divinity. Even though the first party has bee
reduced to silence, whether by the power of truth alone o
also by the impetuosity of the other party, and though the
feel overwhelmed in respect to the fundamentals of the case
they still have not been satisfied regarding their demands: thei
demands are just but have not been fulfilled. Their silence i
only half due to victory—half to the boredom and indifferenc
which are usually the consequences of constantly excited ex
pectations when the promises made are never fulfilled.[16]

Regarding the contents, the others certainly sometime
make it easy enough for themselves to have great spread. The
drag a lot of material into their field, namely material that i
already familiar and well ordered. And when they deal prefer
ably with the queer and curious, they only seem that muc
more to have firm possession of the rest which knowledge ha
long taken care of in its way, as if their mastery of the unrul
came in addition to all this. Thus they subject everything t
the absolute idea which then appears to be recognized i
everything and to have developed into a comprehensive sci
ence. But when this comprehensiveness is considered mor
closely, it becomes manifest that it was not attained insofa
as one and the same principle differentiated itself into differer
forms, but it is rather the formless repetition of one and th
same principle which is merely applied externally to differer
material and thus receives a dull semblance of differentiatior
The idea, true enough by itself, remains in fact just where i
was in the beginning as long as the development consist
merely in such repetition of the same formula. When th
knowing subject applies the one unmoved form to whatever

e romantic circle or a religious denomination. The time for ecial privilege is past.

On the face of it, it is ironical that this insistence on uni- rsal intelligibility should appear in the preface to a work of gendary difficulty which even professionals have the greatest uble in understanding. And after all is said, this irony re- ains striking. But it should be noted that Hegel's position does t commit him to popularization. Science, including higher athematics and advanced physics, is exoteric and democratic the sense here at stake; and Hegel constantly insists that ilosophy requires the most serious exertion and hard work. deed, this is part of what he means when he speaks of evating philosophy to the level of a science.

16 Confronted with such allusions, which turn up roughout the *Phenomenology*, one always has to ask both 10m in particular Hegel had in mind and whether he suc- eded in characterizing recurrent and typical phenomena. ere, "one side" seems to refer to representatives of the En- ghtenment, and "the other side" to some of the romantics. 1807 the romantics were prevailing, but Hegel found the mand for universal intelligibility "just."

The final sentence is very probably directed particularly ainst Friedrich Schlegel, one of the leading spirits of the rly romantic movement in Germany, who aroused great pectations with his bold promises, but who is said to have sappointed his hearers dismally when he came to the Uni- rsity of Jena. (Cf. Hegel's letter of August 2, 1816, in D.) it Schlegel may have been the mere occasion for Hegel's sight into this type of romanticism. "The boredom and in- fference which are usually the consequences of constantly cited expectations when the promises made are never ful- led" could also be documented from the journals of one of helling's students at the University of Berlin, a decade after egel's death. The student was Søren Kierkegaard.

The immediately following polemic ("Regarding the con- 1ts . . .") has often been understood as a critique of the ung Schelling. For a discussion of the question whether me of the polemics in this preface were aimed at Schelling, e H 39; cf. also Hegel's and Schelling's correspondence of 07, translated in D.

is presented, and the material is externally dipped into th resting element, this is not, any more than arbitrary notior about the contents, the fulfillment of that which is in fae required—to wit, the wealth that wells forth out of itself an the self-differentiation of the forms. Rather it is a drab mone chromatic formalism that gets to the differentiation of th material solely because this is long prepared and familiar.

Yet he[17] proclaims this monotony and abstract generalit as the absolute; he assures us that any dissatisfaction with th' is mere incapacity to master the absolute point of view and t abide there. Formerly, the mere possibility that one could als imagine something in another way was sufficient to refute notion,[18] and this same bare possibility, the general though also had the full positive value of actual knowledge. Now her we find that all value is also ascribed to the general idea i this form of non-actuality, while the dissolution of the distin and determinate—or rather the resolve, which is neither d veloped further nor self-justifying, to thrust the distinct an determinate into the abyss of emptiness—is presented as th speculative mode of study.

To study anything as it is in the absolute here means merel that one says of it: to be sure, it has just been spoken of a something, but in the absolute, the A=A, there is nothing c the sort, for in the absolute everything is one. To pit this on piece of information, that in the absolute all is one, against a the distinctions of knowledge, both attained knowledge an the search and demand for knowledge—or to pass off one absolute as the night in which, as one says, all cows are blac —that is the naïveté of the emptiness of knowledge.[19]

Recent philosophy accuses and derogates formalism, an yet formalism has regenerated itself in its very midst. Bi though the inadequacy of formalism is familiar and felt, it wi not disappear from science until the knowledge of absolut actuality has gained perfect clarity about its nature.[20]

Since the general notion, if it precedes an attempt to exe cute it, makes it easier to understand the latter, it may b helpful to offer some suggestions at this point. At the sam time, this occasion may be used to eliminate a few form whose customary acceptance constitutes an obstacle for phi osophical knowledge.

[17] The German pronoun, *er,* could refer—and, no doubt, does, strictly speaking—to "monochromatic formalism." But it is a little difficult to picture this drab formalism as proclaiming things and assuring us, and the German reader who has recognized the portrait of Schelling—or of his typical imitator—is bound to think of *him,* not of *it.*

[18] "imagine": *sich etwas . . . vorzustellen;* "notion": *Vorstellung.* Cf. I.2, note [1] above.

[19] Here are a few pertinent quotations from Schelling's *Bruno* (1802):

"In this absolute unity, however—because in it everything is, as has been shown, perfect and itself absolute—nothing is distinguishable from anything else, for things are distinguished only by their imperfections . . ." (p. 83).

". . . that which is not but which is the ground of existence, the primeval night, the mother of all things" (p. 124).

"He, however, would stray furthest from the idea of the absolute who would determine its nature, in order not to determine it as being, by the concept of activity" (p. 171).

In connection with the preceding pages, the following quotation, too, is relevant:

"And philosophy is necessarily, by its very nature, esoteric . . ." (p. 31). In Schelling's *Werke:* I, IV, pp. 232, 258, 278, 303.

The "A=A" occurs in Schelling's *Darstellung meines Systems der Philosophie* (1801), §§ 4 ff.

See also his "Aphorismen zur Einleitung in die Naturphilosophie" in *Jahrbücher der Medizin als Wissenschaft* (1806): "The absolute therefore can be expressed eternally only as absolute, altogether indivisible identity"; "God is the equally eternal night and the equally eternal day of things" (*Werke,* 1860, vol. VII; 1927, reprinted 1958, vol. IV; #65 and #102).

On the whole question whether Hegel's polemic was directed against Schelling see H 39 and D 1807.

[20] "its nature" probably refers to formalism but could also refer to "the knowledge." No doubt, clarity about the nature of both is important.

5. *The absolute is subject—*

[II.1]

According to my view, which must justify itself[1] by the presentation of the system, everything depends on this, that we comprehend and express the true not as substance but just as much as subject.[2] At the same time it should be noted that substantiality involves the generality or immediacy both of knowledge itself and of that which is being or immediacy *for* knowledge.[3]

Comprehending God as the one substance outraged the age in which this definition was proclaimed.[4] On the one hand, this was due to the instinctive recognition that self-consciousness was only drowned in it and not preserved; on the other hand, however, the opposite view which clings to thinking as thinking is generality as such and the same simplicity or undifferentiated, unmoved substantiality.[5] And when, thirdly, thinking unites with itself the being of the substance and comprehends immediacy or intuition as thinking, it still remains decisive whether this intellectual intuition does not fall back into inert simplicity and present actuality in a non-actual manner.[6]

6. *—and what this is*

The living substance is, further, that being which is in truth subject or—to say the same thing in other words—which is in truth actual only insofar as it is the movement of positing itself, or the mediation between a self and its development into something different. As subject, it is pure, simple negativity[7] and thus the bifurcation of the simple, that which produces its own double and opposition, a process that again negates this indifferent diversity and its opposite: only this sameness which reconstitutes itself, or the reflection into itself in being different—not an original unity as such, or an immedi-

II. *The idea of a phenomenology of the spirit*

1. The true not only substance but also subject

¹ In the second, posthumously published, edition "only" (*nur*) was inserted at this point; and subsequent editions have retained this stylistic horror. Since the beginning of the preface had been revised for a second edition by Hegel just before he died—the point to which he got will be indicated in this commentary—the change was presumably made by him; but if "only" is inserted, "must" should be changed to "can."

² "substance" here remotely resembles Aristotle's matter, and "subject" his form. The two terms allude, respectively, to Spinoza and Fichte, and it is relevant that Fichte had claimed at a time when Spinoza was still in ill repute as an atheist that at bottom there were only two types of philosophy: Spinoza's "Dogmatism" and Fichte's "Idealism."

³ One of Hegel's central ideas: philosophy should deal neither with the modes of knowledge alone nor with the objects alone, but with both in their correlation. Where the absolute is conceived as an undifferentiated, unmediated substance, it will be claimed that the absolute is accessible only to immediate knowledge.

⁴ Spinoza.

⁵ According to Lasson, Kant is meant.

⁶ Schelling.

⁷ Cf. Spinoza's famous *"determinatio negatio est"* Letter 50; June 2, 1674.

ate unity as such—is the true. The true is its own becoming, the circle that presupposes its end as its aim and thus has it for its beginning—that which is actual only through its execution and end.[8]

Thus the life of God and divine knowledge may indeed be spoken of as love's playing with itself; yet this idea descends to the level of edification[9] and even insipidity when seriousness, pain, and the patience and work of the negative have no place in it. In itself[10] this life is indeed unstained sameness and unity with itself which is not serious about otherness, estrangement, and the overcoming of this estrangement. But this in-itself is abstract generality in which the nature of this life to be *for itself*,[10] and thus also the self-movement of the form, are ignored.

When the form is said to be the same as the essence, it is plainly a misunderstanding to suppose that knowledge can be satisfied with the in-itself or the essence while sparing itself concern with the form—as if the absolute principle or the absolute intuition made the explication of the former or the development of the latter dispensable. Precisely because the form is no less essential to the essence than the essence itself, the essence is to be comprehended and spoken of not merely as essence, i.e., as immediate substance or as the pure self-contemplation of the divine, but just as much as form—and in the whole wealth of the developed form. Only in that way is it comprehended and spoken of in its actuality.[11]

⁸ In this paragraph Hegel explains what he means by calling "the true" a "subject." A subject is that which is "actual only insofar as it is the movement of positing itself, or the mediation between a self and its development into something different" (*die Vermittlung des sich anders Werdens mit sich selbst*). These phrases do not merely designate features of being a subject but are introduced: "or—to say the same thing in other words . . ." (*oder was dasselbe heisst*). To elucidate Hegel's meaning it may help to recall the motto which the young Nietzsche derived from Pindar, Pyth. II. 73: *genoi hoios essi,* and which he formulated in his *Gay Science* (§ 270): "You shall become who you are." Much later he subtitled his *Ecce Homo: How one becomes what one is.* What Hegel means by a subject is that which makes itself what it becomes. Cf. Hegel's own formulations in his introductory lectures on the philosophy of history: "Thus the organic individual produces itself: it makes of itself what it is implicitly [*an sich*]; thus the spirit, too, is only that which it makes of itself, and it makes of itself what it is implicitly" (VG 151). Also: "The spirit essentially acts; it makes of itself what it is implicitly—makes itself into its own deed, its own work" (67 L); and "The spirit is essentially the result of its own activity: its activity is transcending of immediacy, negating it, and returning into itself" (72 f. L). Cf. H 60 and ¹² and ¹⁷ below.

⁹ Cf. I.2.9.

¹⁰ "In itself": *an sich.* Often, as in note ⁸ above, what is meant is implicitly or potentially, but here the meaning is almost the opposite: looked at superficially, without regard for its entelechy, or, as Hegel says, ignoring its inner nature. The meaning here accords with both ordinary usage and Kant's precedent (the thing in itself, *das Ding an sich*). *An sich,* like in itself, often means: taken by itself, apart from its relations to other matters, or, in effect, considered superficially. Hegel's usage of this key term of his philosophy is thus not consistent.

The term is often paired by Hegel with "for itself" (*für sich*) which is meant to suggest individuality or, more specifically, both separate being and self-conscious being. This pair of terms has been adopted and adapted by Sartre: *en soi* and *pour soi.*

¹¹ Schelling already had identified form and essence, but in the sense of an undifferentiated identity. Any contrast was due merely to the finite point of view. Hegel, on the other

The true is the whole. But the whole is only the essence perfecting itself through its development. Of the absolute it should be said that it is essentially result, that it is only in the end what it is in truth; and precisely in this consists its nature: to be actual, subject, or that which becomes itself.[12]

Though it may seem contradictory that the absolute is to be comprehended essentially as result, it requires only a little reflection to clear up this semblance of contradiction. The beginning, the principle, or the absolute, as it is spoken of at first and immediately is merely the general. Just as when I say, "all animals," this phrase is not acceptable as a zoology, it is obvious that such words as the divine, absolute, eternal, etc., do not express what they contain. And only such words do indeed express the intuition as something immediate. Whatever is more than such a word, even the transition to a mere proposition, contains a becoming something other which must then be taken back, and is thus a mediation. This, however, is precisely what some people abhor, as if absolute knowledge had been abandoned as soon as one makes more of mediation than to say that it is nothing absolute and that it has no place in the absolute.[13]

This abhorrence, however, is really rooted in ignorance of the nature of both mediation and absolute knowledge. For mediation is nothing else than self-identity that moves itself; or it is reflection into itself, the moment of the ego which is for itself, pure negativity or, reduced to its pure abstraction,[14] simple becoming. The ego or becoming in general—this mediation is on account of its simplicity precisely growing immediacy and the immediate itself.[15]

It is therefore a misapprehension about reason when reflection is excluded from the true instead of being comprehended as a positive moment of the absolute. It is reflection that makes the true a result while also sublimating[16] this opposition to its becoming; for this becoming is also quite simple and therefore not different from the form of the true which manifests itself in the result as something simple: rather it is precisely this return into simplicity.

While the embryo is surely in itself human, it still is not human for itself: human for itself is only the educated reason

hand, insists that philosophy must not concern itself exclusively with the undifferentiated essence [*Wesen*], which he equates with the in-itself; it must also try to comprehend the forms in which this essence reveals itself and through which it develops.

[12] Cf. note [8] above; also I.1, note [6] on the proper approach to philosophy. Hegel's insistence that the absolute is subject as well as substance may at first seem less heretical than Spinoza's position; but here it becomes perfectly plain that Hegel's conception is no less heretical though in a different way.

[13] One might communicate immediate knowledge by exclaiming "God!" But as soon as we describe the content of knowledge in a sentence we differentiate and depart from immediacy: we name the one (the subject) and the other (the predicate) and then simultaneously cancel and preserve this differentiation when we mediate between the two and assert the predicate of the subject. The result is no longer an undifferentiated and immediate simplicity.

[14] These five words, absent from the first edition, were inserted by Hegel when he prepared a revised edition. Most of his other revisions were even slighter, and it is surely astonishing that he did not succeed at all in making his extraordinarily difficult preface clearer and more readable.

[15] Hegel again suggests that the mode of knowledge corresponds to its object: propositional knowledge does not involve a fall from grace in which the object is betrayed. The absolute itself is a differentiated unity—not an unstained essence but a subject that lives and becomes what it is.

[16] "sublimate" is here employed throughout to render *aufheben*. Further on in the *Phenomenology*, near the beginning of the discussion of perception (*Die Wahrnehmung*) Hegel explains: "*Das Aufheben* exhibits its true double meaning which we have observed in the negative: it negates and at the same time preserves." Cf. H 34 and 42.

which has made itself that which it is in itself.[17] Only this is its actuality. But this result is itself simple immediacy[18]; for it is self-conscious freedom which rests in itself and has not laid opposition aside to let it lie there, but is reconciled to it.

What has been said here can also be expressed by saying that reason is purposive activity. The elevation of what is supposed to be nature above thinking, which is also misunderstood, and especially the banishment of external purposiveness, have brought the form of purpose in general into disrepute.[19] Yet even as Aristotle, too, defines nature as purposive activity, purpose is the immediate, that which is at rest, the unmoved mover; thus it is subject.[20] Its power to move, taken abstractly, is being-for-itself or pure negativity. The result is the same as the beginning only because the beginning is purpose. In other words, the actual is the same as its Concept only because the immediate, being purpose, contains the self or pure actuality in itself. The executed purpose or the actual as existent is movement and unfolded becoming; but precisely this unrest is the self. And it is like the immediacy and simplicity of the beginning because it is the result, that which has returned into itself—and that which has returned into itself is the self, and the self is the identity and simplicity that relates itself to itself.[21]

The need to represent the absolute as subject has employed the propositions: God is what is eternal, or the moral world order, or love, and so forth. In such propositions the true is only posited straightway as the subject, but it is not represented as the movement of that which reflects itself into itself. In a proposition of this kind one begins with the word God. This by itself is a senseless sound, a mere name; only the predicate says what he is and fills the name with content and meaning; the empty beginning becomes actual knowledge only in this end. For this reason, it is not clear why they do not speak merely of the eternal, of the moral world order, and so forth —or as the ancients did, of pure Concepts, such as being, the One, and so forth—in sum, only of that which supplies the meaning, without adding the senseless sound as well. But this word signifies that what is posited is not a being or essence or

[17] See note [10] above. This passage helps us to understand Hegel's terminology.

[18] A result, though mediated, can be perceived immediately, all at once, as a simple datum. Cf. H 44.

[19] Hegel is referring to Kant's critique of that external teleology which claims, for example, that it is the purpose of the cork to furnish stoppers for our bottles.

[20] In the first edition: ". . . that which is at rest and is mover or subject." The revision is Hegel's.

[21] Kierkegaard's *Sickness unto Death* begins (not counting the prefatory matter) with an extraordinarily difficult passage in which he argues at length that the self as a mere synthesis of the finite and infinite, body and soul, etc., is not yet a self, and that what really defines a self is its relation to itself. Much of his book is a catalogue of bad attitudes toward oneself: what he calls despair and what others might prefer to call attempts to escape from oneself or *mauvaise foi*. Some of Kierkegaard's expositors assume that the synthesis view of the self which Kierkegaard attacks is Hegel's—usually they also assume, falsely, that Hegel constantly talks of theses, antitheses, and syntheses—but in fact the view which Kierkegaard offers as his own is taken straight from this paragraph of the *Phenomenology*.

Many of Kierkegaard's expositors assume further that his insistence on "subjective" truth must be contrasted with Hegel's supposed belief that religion is a matter of propositions. In the following paragraph Hegel discusses the inadequacy of propositions about God.

mere generality, but rather something reflected into itself—a subject. Yet at the same time this is only anticipated. The subject is accepted as a fixed point to which the predicates are affixed as to their support—by a movement which belongs to those who know of the subject and which is not supposed to belong to the fixed point—though only this [recognition][22] could represent the content as a subject. In the way in which the movement is here constituted, it could not belong to the point; but after this point has been presupposed it really cannot be constituted differently and is bound to be merely external. This anticipation that the absolute is subject is therefore not only not the actuality of this Concept but even makes this actuality impossible; for it posits a point at rest, while the actuality is self-movement.[23]

Among several implications of what has here been said, one may be singled out for special emphasis: it is only as science or system that knowledge is actual[24] and can be expounded. Further, any so-called basic proposition or principle of philosophy, if true, is also false simply insofar as it is merely[25] a basic proposition or principle.

It is therefore easy to refute it. The refutation consists in demonstrating its deficiency; and it is deficient because it is

²² "this": namely, the recognition that the movement belongs to the supposedly fixed point. Hegel's sentence is elliptical, and he did not improve it when he made many other unhelpful revisions. Strictly speaking, his pronoun, *sie* (here rendered as "this" on account of its emphatic position—the German reads *durch sie aber wäre allein*) can refer back only to "a movement . . ."

²³ Although traditional theology anticipates Hegel's insight that the absolute is subject—or, speaking more idiomatically, that God resembles a self—the form of this anticipation is really incompatible with that which is anticipated. Traditional theology is not completely irrational; it has a premonition of the truth; but when this truth is disentangled from the web of traditional theology, the web is broken. Hegel argues that in theology "God" is treated as a subject at rest whose nature we all know even before we are informed that "God is love"; but in fact we do not know the absolute to begin with, and apart from the development of the concepts that are here offered as predicates God cannot be known and does not know himself. Cf. notes ¹² and ⁸ above.

²⁴ *dass das Wissen* (knowledge) *nur als Wissenschaft* (science) *oder als System wirklich ist* . . .

Hegel's idea of science is obviously very different from Nietzsche's or the logical positivists'. Nietzsche, the author of *The Gay Science* (*Fröhliche Wissenschaft*) stressed open-mindedness, freedom from moral and religious preconceptions, and bold experimentalism. Other philosophers have stressed close attention to empirical fact and the importance of the verifiability of claims. Hegel says "science or system" and opposes his view on the one hand to those who extol feeling and intuition while disparaging the articulateness of propositions, and on the other hand to those who place their trust in a few fundamental propositions or dogmas. What is needed, according to Hegel, is a systematic and comprehensive analysis of concepts.

²⁵ "insofar as it is merely": Hegel's revision of the first edition which read "because it is . . ." This change is a slight improvement.

Hegel took up this polemic and developed it in his *Encyclopedia* (1817, §§ 14 ff.; 1827, §§ 28 ff.; and in definitive form in the 3d edition of 1830, §§ 26–36; indeed, the following sections down through 78 are of the utmost interest in connection with the preface to the *Phenomenology*). See, for exam-

merely general or a principle—the mere beginning. If the ref
utation is thorough, it is taken and developed out of the prin
ciple itself—and not effected externally by opposite assurance:
and notions.[26] Thus it would really be the development of
this principle and the completion of its deficiency, if only the
refutation would not misunderstand itself by paying attention
solely to its negative activity without also becoming conscious
of its progress and results on their positive side.

The positive explication of the beginning is at the same time
also, conversely, a negative treatment of it insofar as it is
directed against the one-sided form of the beginning which is
only immediate or purpose. Therefore it can also be taken for
a refutation of that which constitutes the basis of the system,
but it would be more correct to look upon it as a demonstration that the basis or the principle of the system is in fact only
its beginning.

That the true is actual only as system, or that the substance
is essentially subject, is expressed in the conception which
speaks of the absolute as spirit.[27] This is the most sublime
Concept, and it belongs to the modern age and its religion.
The spiritual alone is the actual[28]; it is [i] the essence of
being-in-itself; [ii] that which relates itself and is determinate,
that which is other and for itself; and [iii] that which in this
determinateness and being outside itself remains in itself—or,
in other words, it is in and for itself.

This being-in-and-for-itself, however, it is first for us or in
itself: it is the spiritual substance. Then it must also become
this for itself and attain the knowledge of the spiritual and of
itself as the spirit; i.e., it must become an object for itself, but
just as immediately an object which is sublimated,[29] reflected
into itself. It is for itself only for us, insofar as its spiritual
content is generated by it itself. But insofar as it is for itself
also for itself, this self-generation, the pure Concept is for it
at the same time the objective element in which it has its existence; and in this way it is in its existence for itself an object
reflected into itself.[30]

The spirit that, so developed, knows itself as spirit is science.
Science is the actuality of the spirit and the realm that the
spirit builds for itself in its own element.

ple, the last sentence of § 28 (1830): "One failed to inquire whether such predicates were in and for themselves something true, and whether the form of the judgment could be the form of truth." And the end of § 31: "the judgment is through its form one-sided and insofar false."

[26] This commendation of internal criticism, though original, owes something to the practice of Fichte vis-à-vis Kant, and of Schelling vis-à-vis both: whatever one may think of their work—and Kant disowned Fichte; and Fichte, Schelling —these men tried to remedy deficiencies in their predecessors.

[27] In view of the following sentence, even Baillie has to write "Spirit" here, as indeed he has to again and again because "spirit" is so plainly right and "mind" impossible; and yet Baillie's translation bears the title *The Phenomenology of Mind,* and often he translates *Geist* as mind. Cf. H 34 and 65.

[28] See I.3, note [6] above, and cf. Hegel's famous dictum in the preface to the *Philosophy of Right* (1821): "What is rational, is actual; and what is actual, is rational." Some of Hegel's detractors have claimed that this view was improvised to please the King of Prussia, as Hegel was by then a professor at the University of Berlin, but here we find the same view expressed in almost the same words in 1807.

The Roman numerals in brackets are not found in any of the early editions and have been added to help the reader.

[29] See note [16] above. The first edition read: "an object which is mediated, i.e., sublimated . . ." Hegel's revision.

[30] "in itself" and "for itself": see note [10] above. "In and for itself": *an und für sich* is a common German idiom with a minimum of meaning, really little more than a slightly more elegant equivalent of the "ah" and "er" with which some people sprinkle public speeches. Hegel employs this phrase as a technical term and defines it, under [iii]. "For us or in itself": the embryo is human only in itself and for us, not yet for itself. The infant is "for itself only for us."

7. The element of knowledge

[II.2]

Pure self-recognition in absolute otherness, this ether as such, is the ground and basis of science or knowledge in general. The beginning of philosophy presupposes or demands that consciousness dwell in this element.[1] But this element itself receives its perfection and transparence only through the movement of its becoming. It is pure spirituality as[2] the general that has the manner of simple immediacy[3]; this simple, as it has existence as such, is the basis that is thinking and only in the spirit. Because this element, this immediacy of the spirit, is the very substance of the spirit, it is the transfigured essence and the reflection which itself is simple and immediacy as such for itself—being that is reflection into itself. Science on her part demands of self-consciousness[4] that it should have elevated itself into this ether to be able to live—and to live—with her and in her. Conversely, the individual has the right to demand that science should at least furnish him with the ladder to this standpoint[5]—and show him this standpoint within himself. His right is based on his absolute independence which he possesses in every form of his knowledge; for in all of them, whether they are recognized by science or not and regardless of their contents, the individual is the absolute form, i.e., he is the[6] immediate certainty of himself and, if this expression should be preferred, he is therefore unconditioned being. It is the standpoint of consciousness to know of objective things in opposition to itself, and to know of itself in opposition to them. Science considers this standpoint as the other—and precisely that through which consciousness knows itself to be[7] at home with itself is for science the loss of the spirit.[8] Conversely, the element of science is for consciousness a distant beyond in which consciousness no longer has possession of itself. Each of these two appears to the other as the perversion of truth. That the natural consciousness immediately entrusts itself to science is an attempt it makes, attracted

II.2: What is phenomenology?

¹ Confronted with the works of past philosophers, I should make their thought my own and criticize them by taking their ideas more seriously, if possible, than they themselves did. I must not remain at rest as if I witnessed a spectacle and let the ideas be presented to me while I sit back and watch their procession. I have to understand the other as a manifestation of what I myself am, too: spirit.

² "as": first edition had "or." Hegel made many small changes in this paragraph.

³ The following half sentence was not in the first edition, and the next sentence originally read: "Because it is the immediacy of the spirit, because the substance is the spirit, it is the transfigured essence, the reflection which itself is simple or immediacy, being that is reflection into itself."

⁴ First edition: *Die Wissenschaft von ihrer Seite verlangt vom Selbstbewusstsein . . .* Revised version: *Die Wissenschaft verlangt von ihrer Seite an das Selbstbewusstsein . . .* The meaning remains unchanged, the style is worsened.

⁵ The ladder that leads from "Sense Certainty . . . and Opinion" (Chapter I) to "Absolute Knowledge" in the last chapter is the *Phenomenology*. The image of the ladder that leads into the ether may have been suggested by Jacob's dream in Genesis 28:12. Philosophers who have used a similar image include Sextus Empiricus and Wittgenstein, at the end of his *Tractatus*.

The following half sentence was not in the first edition, and the addition impairs the passage.

⁶ "i.e., he is the": the first edition said instead, "or has."

⁷ "knows itself to be": the first edition said, "is."

⁸ Ordinary consciousness defines its own standpoint in opposition to the ideas of others and, as it were, feels at home when it says, "as for me, . . ." But this is a sub-philosophic view (Hegel now uses "science" as a synonym for "philosophy"): see note ¹ above.

by it knows not what, to walk for once also on its head.[9] The compulsion to adopt this unaccustomed position and to move in it amounts to the presumption that the natural consciousness should do itself violence in a manner as unexpected as it must seem unnecessary.

Whatever science may be in itself,[10] in relation to immediate self-consciousness it presents itself as something topsy-turvy. Or: because immediate self-consciousness[11] has the principle of its actuality in its certainty of itself, science bears the form of unactuality for this immediate self-consciousness which seems to itself to stand outside science. Science must therefore join this element[12] to herself,[13] or rather she must show that and how it belongs to her. As long as she lacks such actuality, she is merely the content as[14] the in-itself, the purpose which is still only something inward—not yet spirit, only spiritual substance. This in-itself[15] has to express itself and become for itself; in other words, it[16] has to posit self-consciousness as one with itself.

8. The ascent into this is the Phenomenology of the Spirit

This becoming of science in general or of knowledge is what this phenomenology of the spirit[17] represents. Knowledge in its initial form, or immediate spirit, is that which lacks spirit,[18] the consciousness of the senses. To become true knowledge, or to generate the element of science which is her pure Concept itself,[19] it has to work its way through a long journey.

This becoming, as it will[20] appear in its content and the forms that will[20] show themselves in it, will[20] not be anything like what one would at first associate with an introduction to science for the unscientific consciousness. It will also be quite different from a foundation of science. Above all, it will differ from that enthusiasm which, as shot from a pistol, begins immediately with absolute knowledge, having done with other standpoints simply by declaring that it will not deign to take notice of them.

⁹ This passage undoubtedly prompted Karl Marx's famous remark that is usually misquoted as if he had boasted that he had stood Hegel on his head (even R. G. Collingwood, *The Idea of History*, p. 124, says "upside down"), as if that were anything to boast of. What Marx actually said in the preface to the second edition of *Das Kapital* (1873) was that Hegel's dialectic stands on its head (as if the spirit were fundamental) and must be stood right side up again.

"for once": *auch einmal*. Baillie's "all at once" must be due to his confusing this phrase with *auf einmal*. His "attempt, induced by some unknown influence, all at once to walk on its head" quite misses Hegel's sudden whimsey.

¹⁰ "in itself": *an ihr selbst*. A solecism often used by Hegel in place of *an sich* or *an sich selbst*. Usually, as here, he intended meaning is the same: taken by itself, apart from its relations.

¹¹ The revised version says only "the same"; the first edition: "because immediate self-consciousness is the principle of actuality, science bears . . ."

¹² First edition: *jenes Element;* revision: *solches Element.*

¹³ "herself": to insure clarity without excessive clumsiness it seemed best to use the feminine pronoun for science, as in German.

¹⁴ "the content as": missing in the first edition.

¹⁵ "This in-itself": first edition had *sie* (it) which could mean science or the spiritual substance.

¹⁶ "it" (first edition) later changed to "the same."

¹⁷ After "spirit" Hegel struck out several words of the first edition: "as the first part of the system of the same." "The same" means science. On the original title page, "System of Science, First Part" had preceded the present title.

¹⁸ After "spirit" Hegel deleted "or is."

¹⁹ "itself": missing in first edition. The following "it" was originally *er* and referred to the spirit; now it is *es* and may be meant to refer all the way back to the consciousness of the senses (*das sinnliche Bewusstsein*). Again the original text is impaired.

²⁰ In the original edition this sentence was cast in the present tense. Regardless of its tense, this is surely one of the least controversial sentences in Hegel's works.

[II.3]

The task of leading the individual from his uneducated standpoint to knowledge had to be taken in its general sense, and the general individual, the self-conscious spirit,[1] had to be considered in its education.

As for the relation of the two: in the general individual every moment shows itself as it gains concrete form and its own shape. The particular individual is the incomplete spirit, a concrete form in whose whole existence one determination predominates,[2] while the others are present only in blurred features. In the spirit who stands on a higher level than another, the lower concrete existence has been reduced to an insignificant moment; what formerly was the matter itself has become a mere trace; its form is shrouded and become a simple shade.

Through this past the individual whose substance is the spirit that stands on a higher level passes in the same manner in which the student of a higher science goes once more through the preparatory knowledge that he has long mastered, to present the contents to his mind: he recalls these memories without being interested in them for their own sake or wishing to abide in them. The individual must also pass through the contents of the educational stages of the general spirit, but as forms that have long been outgrown by the spirit, as stages of a way that has been prepared and evened for him.[3] Thus we see that as far as information is concerned, what in former ages occupied the mature spirits of men has been reduced to information, exercises, and even games suitable for boyhood; and in the boy's pedagogical progress we recognize the history of the education of the world as if it had been traced in a silhouette.[4] This past existence is property that has already been acquired by the general spirit which constitutes the substance of the individual[5] and, by thus appearing to him externally, his inorganic nature.

In this respect, education, considered from the point of view of the individual, consists in his acquiring what is thus given to him; he must digest his inorganic nature and take possession

II.3: Whose spirit? Individual or universal?

[1] Instead of "the self-conscious spirit" the first edition had *der Weltgeist,* the world spirit; "education": *Bildung.*

[2] The first edition had: "a concrete form whose whole existence is given over to . . ."

Each philosopher represents above all one principle, one attitude, one point of view; and insofar as any individual has his own outlook, one aspect predominates though other positions may be discernible in his views, if only in blurred features. Are all men on the same level, then? No, some are more advanced: their vision is more inclusive and incorporates the partial insights of those who remain on a lower level.

[3] This is Hegel's ontogenetic principle and his answer to the question whether he is concerned with the spirit of the individual or with the *Weltgeist:* even as the embryo has to recapitulate in abbreviated form the stages of organic evolution, the individual spirit must recapitulate in condensed form the *Bildung* of the human spirit.

[4] N.B.: "as far as information is concerned." Hegel has not changed his mind about what he wrote in an early fragment in which he scorned the remark "that today any small child knows more about God than the wisest pagan" and insisted on the importance of "consciousness gained through experience" (Nohl, 11; quoted at length and discussed in WK 132).

"silhouette": without any depth and greatly oversimplified.

[5] Instead of the following seven words the first edition had "or." The "which" in this sentence can refer only to the general spirit. "Inorganic nature" until it is consumed, absorbed, and digested, and thus becomes part of our spiritual organism.

of it for himself.[6] But from the point of view of the general spirit as the substance this means nothing else than that this should acquire self-consciousness and produce its becoming and reflection in itself.[7]

Science represents this educational movement both in its detail and necessity and also as that which has already been reduced to a moment and property of the spirit. The aim is the spirit's insight into what constitutes knowledge. Impatience demands the impossible, namely the attainment of the aim without the means. First, the length of this way must be endured, for every moment is necessary.[8] Secondly, one must take time over every one, for each is itself an individual and entire form and is considered absolutely insofar as one considers its determinateness as something whole and concrete, or the whole in the individuality of this determination.[9]

Because the substance of the individual, because[10] the world spirit has had the patience to pass through these forms in the long expanse of time, taking upon itself the tremendous labor of world history[11] in which it imparted as much of its content to every form as that form was capable of holding, and because it could not attain consciousness about itself with less labor, therefore the individual cannot in the nature of the case[12] comprehend his own substance with less than this; and yet he has less trouble because this is already accomplished in itself: the content is by now the actuality reduced to a possibility, vanquished immediacy,[13] and the forms have been reduced to abbreviations and to the simple determinations of thought. Having already been thought, the content is the possession of the substance.[14] No longer must existence be transformed into the in-itself; only the in-itself—which is neither raw any more, nor immersed in existence, but rather something recalled—needs to be transmuted into the form of the for-itself. How this is to be done[15] must now be described in some detail.

9. The transmutation of the notion and the familiar into thought—[16]

What is no longer necessary at the point at which we are here taking up this movement[17] is the sublimation of exist-

⁶ Cf. Goethe's *Faust,* lines 682 f.: "What from your fathers you received as heir, / Acquire if you would possess it." Hegel's choice of words is strikingly similar, and this quotation would furnish a fitting motto for his book; but Goethe's lines did not appear in *Faust: A Fragment* (1790) and were published only in 1808 when the whole of Part One came out, a year after the *Phenomenology.* The lines were written much earlier, and it is possible that Hegel had heard them somehow. The minute differences between the wordings of Hegel's sentence in the first and second edition do not affect this point.

⁷ This sentence read in the first edition: "But this means nothing else than that the general spirit or the substance should acquire self-consciousness or its becoming and reflection in itself." The general spirit or *Weltgeist,* it should be noted, acquires self-consciousness only through us. So far is Hegel from theism.

⁸ "necessary": see I.1, end of note ⁶ above.

⁹ Here Hegel does not only defend the length of the *Phenomenology;* he also insists on the dignity of every single stage, "for each is itself an individual and entire form."

¹⁰ After "because" the revised version inserts "even" (*sogar*), another impairment. In the original text we are reminded that the world spirit *is* the substance of the individual.

¹¹ The following clause, down to the comma, was not in the first edition.

¹² "in . . . case": not in the original edition, nor an improvement.

¹³ The remainder of this sentence was not in the first edition.

¹⁴ "substance": the first edition had "individual."

¹⁵ First edition: the parenthesis in the previous sentence and the period at the end were missing, and in place of "how . . . done" it had "which."

¹⁶ *Verwandlung des Vorgestellten und Bekannten in den Gedanken.* On *vorstellen* see I.2, note ¹ above. The German seems to equate the notion and the familiar; and what is meant is below the level of thought and, *a fortiori,* of the Concept.

The next heading is elliptical and presupposes this one.

¹⁷ First edition: "What of this movement is no longer necessary for the individual is . . ."

ence. But what remains[18] and still requires a higher trans-
formation is the notion of and familiarity with the forms.
Existence, taken back into the substance, has merely been
transposed immediately by this first negation into the element
of the self. This possession which the self has acquired[19] thus
still has the same character of uncomprehended immediacy
and unmoved difference as does existence itself: all this is
retained in the notion.

At the same time it is thus something familiar, something
that the existing[20] spirit has mastered so that its activity and
interest no longer abide in it. The activity that masters existence is itself only the movement[21] of the particular spirit
which does not comprehend itself; but knowledge is directed
against the notion that arises in this way, against this familiarity: knowledge is the activity of the general self and the interest of thinking.

What is familiar is not known simply because it is familiar.[22] It is the most common self-deception and deception of
others to presuppose something as familiar when it comes to
knowledge, and to accept this; but with all its talking back and
forth such knowledge, without knowing what is happening to
it, never gets anywhere. The subject and object, etc., God,
nature, the understanding, the sensibility, etc., are presupposed
as familiar and valid foundations without having been scruti-
nized, and they are accepted as fixed points of both departure
and return.[23] They remain unmoved as one moves back and
forth between them—and thus only on their surfaces. Thus
apprehension and examination, too, consist merely in seeing
whether everybody finds what has been said of them in his
notion, too, whether it seems and is familiar to him that way
or not.[24]

The analysis of a notion, as it used to be performed, was
nothing else than the sublimation[25] of the form of its familiarity. Dissecting a notion into its original elements means
going back to its moments which at least do not have the form
of the notion encountered as a datum, constituting rather the
immediate property of the self. To be sure, this analysis only
reaches thoughts which are themselves familiar, fixed, and

¹⁸ The next six words were not in the first edition.

¹⁹ Instead of the first seven words of this sentence the first edition had simply "it," which referred to existence.

²⁰ "existing": not in the first edition.

²¹ Instead of "is itself only the movement," the first edition had: "is the immediate or existing mediation and thus the movement only . . ."

Hegel's revision of the text had got only to the end of this paragraph when he died in 1831.

²² This is one of Hegel's best epigrams: *Das Bekannte überhaupt ist darum, weil es bekannt ist, nicht erkannt.* This is not a pun but a reminder that there are at least two kinds of knowledge which should not be confused: what is known by acquaintance and familiar (*bekannt*) is not necessarily known in the sense of being comprehended (*erkannt*). In one sense we know our acquaintances, in another we often don't. Hegel's power of expression is often considerable, but he very rarely manages to be so brief and concise.

²³ This is perhaps Hegel's most central criticism of other approaches to philosophy, developed at great length in his *Encyclopedia* (1830, §§ 26–78): they fail to analyze such key terms or Concepts as those enumerated here.

²⁴ "apprehension and examination": *Auffassen und Prüfen.* The former could mean "understanding," but here plainly refers to something vaguer. The latter cannot mean "proving" as Baillie renders it. As an extreme illustration of what Hegel here criticizes one may recall Dr. Johnson's famous claim that he could refute Berkeley's idealism simply by kicking a stone. Dr. Johnson appealed to a familiar experience and, without realizing that he presupposed anything controversial, did presuppose a particular interpretation of that experience. But Hegel's critique embraces all kinds of common sense philosophies as well as every scholasticism that stops short of a thorough analysis of the concepts it uses.

²⁵ Here cancellation is the dominant sense, but some degree of preservation is present, too.

static determinations. But what is thus differentiated and unactual is itself an essential moment; for it is only because the
concrete differentiates itself and makes itself what is unactual,
that it is that which moves itself. The activity of differentiating
is the strength and work of the understanding, which is the
most astonishing and the greatest, or rather the absolute,
power.[26]

The circle that rests closed in itself and, being substance,
holds its moments, is the immediate and therefore not per-
plexing relation. But that the accidental as such, separated
from its circumference, that the bounded which is actual only
in its connection with others, should gain an existence of its
own and separate freedom, this is the tremendous power of
the negative; this is the energy of thought, of the pure ego.[27]
Death, if we care to call this unactuality by this name, is
what is most terrible, and to hold on to what is dead requires
the greatest strength. That beauty[28] which lacks strength hates
the understanding because it asks this of her and she cannot
do it. But not the life that shrinks from death and keeps itself
undefiled by devastation, but the life that endures, and preserves itself through, death is the life of the spirit.[29] Spirit
gains its truth only by finding itself in absolute dismemberment.[30] This power it is not as the positive that looks away
from the negative—as when we say of something, this is nothing or false, and then, finished with it, turn away from it to
something else: the spirit is this power only by looking the
negative in the face and abiding with it. This abiding is the
magic force which converts the negative into being.

It is the same which above was called the subject which, by
giving determinateness existence in its element, sublimates abstract immediacy—i.e., immediacy which barely *is*—and thus is
true substance: that being or that immediacy which does not
leave mediation outside itself but which is mediation itself.[31]

10. —and this into the Concept[16]

That notions become the property of pure self-consciousness, this elevation to generality is only one side and not yet

²⁶ Analysis dissects the familiar form and brings to light elements or moments that were not given, not data, but are in a sense the creatures of the mind. Yet the moments which we discriminate and which seem unactual insofar as they have no separate existence in the world are essential to what is analyzed. Cf. II.1, notes ³ and ¹⁵ above. Hegel's encomium on man's analytical powers in the final sentence of this paragraph is striking.

²⁷ Analytic thought does not rest content with unperplexing, familiar, immediately given experiences, things, or concepts: it penetrates the surface (perhaps a three-dimensional image is a little easier to understand than Hegel's two-dimensional circle) and brings to light the bones, muscles, and organs—parts that never had a separate existence before and, in the case of paintings or ideas, even elements that are as much constituted as discovered by thought.

²⁸ *Die kraftlose Schönheit hasst den Verstand* . . . : Baillie's "Beauty, powerless and helpless, hates understanding" is grammatically possible but shows no comprehension of Hegel. Beauty which does *not* lack strength—say, the beauty of a late Rembrandt portrait—can abide analysis, which only brings to light more and more of its excellence.

²⁹ Probably an allusion to the crucifixion and resurrection.

³⁰ An allusion to Dionysus Zagreus who (this is the meaning of "Zagreus") was dismembered—but who is ever reborn. Conceivably, we should also feel reminded of Kant's dismemberment of the spirit in his three *Critiques*.

³¹ Hegel closely associates the following terms: negative, determinateness, subject, mediation, and understanding —and juxtaposes, on the other side, substance, immediate, and intuition. In the paragraph before this, Hegel proceeds from the understanding to dismemberment (*Zerrissenheit*), because the analytic understanding tears its objects apart; and thence to the negative, because the understanding negates and does away with the familiar form of that which it analyzes. The understanding eliminates immediacy and introduces determinations and mediation. Cf. the Schiller quotation in I.2, note ⁵ above. Mediation is required to make what is *bekannt* also *erkannt*. Analysis gives way to a higher immediacy: one might call it a mediated immediacy, but Hegel calls it "that immediacy which does not leave mediation outside itself but which is mediation itself."

the completed education.[32]—Study in antiquity differed from that current in modern times: it was nothing less than the thorough education of the natural consciousness. Testing itself against every separate part of its existence, and philosophizing about everything it encountered, it made itself into a generality that was active through and through.[33] In modern times, on the other hand, the individual finds the abstract form ready-made: the exertion of grasping it and appropriating it is rather more the unmediated production of the inward and the cut-off generation of the general than the emergence of the general out of the concrete and the multiplicity of existence.[34] The work cut out for us now, therefore, is less to purify the individual from the manner of immediacy and the senses while making it into a thinking and thought substance, than to attempt the opposite: to sublimate fixed, determinate thoughts and thus to actualize the general and infuse it with spirit. But it is far more difficult to make fixed thoughts fluid than sense existence.[35] The reason for this has been mentioned above: the substance and the element of existence of these determinations is the ego, the power of the negative, or pure actuality; but the element of the sense determinations is merely powerless, abstract immediacy, or being as such. Thoughts become fluid when pure thinking, this inner immediacy, recognizes itself as a moment, or when pure self-certainty abstracts from itself—not by leaving itself out or setting itself aside, but by abandoning the fixity of its self-positing—both the fixity of the pure concreteness which characterizes the ego even in its opposition to differentiated content and the fixity of differentiations which, posited in the element of pure thinking, share in the unconditionality of the ego.[36] Through this movement the pure thoughts become Concepts and come to be what they are in truth: self-movements, circles, that which is their substance, spiritual entities.[37]

This movement of the pure entities constitutes the nature of what is scientific.[38] As far as the coherence of the contents is concerned, it means the necessity and elaboration of the contents into an organic whole. The way in which the Concept of knowledge is reached thus also becomes a necessary and complete becoming. Hence this preparation ceases to be a fortui-

[32] Self-consciousness, by analysis, dissects subjective notions into universal elements; but this is not enough.

[33] An allusion, above all, to Socrates and Plato.

[34] An allusion to Kant and an implicit criticism of Kant's deduction of the categories in the *Critique of Pure Reason:* instead of painstakingly working his way up to Concepts, like the Greeks, Kant found his categories ready-made in the traditional classification of judgments. This discovery was "un-mediated" and sudden, the deduction "cut-off" and incomplete.

[35] The task confronting Hegel, then, is no longer that which confronted Socrates and Plato; it no longer requires any great effort to raise those interested in philosophy to the level of contemplating Concepts. The task now is no longer to show that the content of sense experience is fluid, as the Greeks from Heraclitus to Plato showed, but, as "is far more difficult, to make fixed thoughts fluid." See I.1, note [5] above, where this image ("fluid") was first mentioned. That Plato in his *Parmenides* had preceded Hegel on this road, too, is duly acknowledged by Hegel later in the preface.

[36] The concepts that Kant, for example (though he is not mentioned specifically), accepted as fixed and rigid and final, as if they required no further analysis and were self-sufficient, must be analyzed painstakingly and will then be seen not to be self-sufficient but essentially interrelated; for example, reality, negation, causality, existence, substance, simple, finite and infinite, free and necessary. This is what Hegel attempted in his *Logic.* But a similar point may be made about Kant's moral philosophy: he treated the bifurcation of reason and inclination as something fixed and thought he offered a timeless analysis of human nature, though in fact he gave us an analysis of only one form of moral consciousness, one *Gestalt des Bewusstseins,* one manifestation of the spirit, one episode in the *Phenomenology of the Spirit*—that which Hegel calls *Moralität* and distinguishes from *Sittlichkeit.* Regarding Hegel's break with Kant over this point, see WK 154 ff.

[37] Only when such concepts—or as Hegel might say, thoughts—as have been enumerated in the previous note are analyzed and considered in their interrelations, only when their fixity gives way in this manner to fluidity, do they become worthy of being called Concepts (*Begriffe*).

[38] "what is scientific": rather, what Hegel calls scientific. Cf. II.1, note [24] above.

tous bit of philosophizing that takes off from these or those objects, relationships, and thoughts of the imperfect consciousness, depending on fortuitous circumstances, nor does it seek to establish what is true by reasoning back and forth, inferring and drawing consequences from determinate thoughts. Rather this way will encompass, by virtue of the movement of the Concept, the complete worldliness of consciousness in its necessity.

Such a presentation constitutes the first part of science because the existence of the spirit is at first nothing else than the immediate or the beginning, but the beginning is not yet its return into itself. The element of immediate existence is therefore that which distinguishes this part of science from the others.[39]—The indication of this difference leads us into a discussion of a few fixed thoughts which usually crop up in this connection.

[39] "the first part of science": i.e., the *Phenomenology of the Spirit* which was published as *System of Science, First Part*. The other parts referred to are Hegel's Logic, his philosophy of nature, and his philosophy of spirit. The claims made for the *Phenomenology* in the preceding passage are open to question, and the claim of "necessity" is certainly untenable. Cf. I.1, note [6] above.

[III.1]

The immediate existence of the spirit, i.e., consciousness, contains the two moments of knowledge and the objectivity which is negative to knowledge.[1] It is in this element [of consciousness] that the spirit develops itself and explicates its moments which are therefore characterized by this opposition and, without exception, appear as forms of consciousness. The science of this way is the science of the experience made by consciousness:[2] the substance is studied insofar as it and its movement are objects of consciousness. Consciousness knows and comprehends nothing but what lies within its experience; for what is within that is only the spiritual substance —specifically, as the object of its self. The spirit, however, becomes an object, for the spirit is this movement of becoming something other for itself, i.e., an object for its self, and then to sublimate this otherhood.[3] And experience is the name we give to just this movement in which the immediate, the unexperienced, i.e., the abstract, whether of sensible being or of a bare, simple thought, becomes estranged and then returns to itself from estrangement, and is only then presented in its actuality and truth and becomes the property of consciousness.[4]

The non-identity we find in consciousness between the ego and the substance that is its object, is their difference, the negative in general. It can be considered as the defect of both, but is really their soul or that which moves them. Therefore some of the ancients comprehended the void as that which moves, seeing well that that which moves is the negative, but not yet that it is the self.

When the negative thus appears at first as the non-identity of the ego and its object, it is just as much the non-identity of the substance with itself. What seems to happen outside it, as an activity directed against it, is its own doing; and thus the substance shows that it is essentially subject. When it has shown this completely, the spirit has made its existence equal to its essence; it becomes an object for itself as it is, and the abstract element of immediacy and of the separation of knowledge

III. Truth

1. The forms of consciousness and truth

[1] "immediate": "Consciousness" is the topic of the first part of the *Phenomenology* which is then followed by "Self-Consciousness" and "Reason." Consciousness does not have the benefit of any previous analysis or reflection; it lacks mediation. The first of the three phases of consciousness that are considered in the first part is "Sense Certainty"—the most naïve type of consciousness. But even at this stage there is some differentiation or, as Hegel here puts it, there are two moments: "knowledge and the objectivity which is negative to knowledge." The odd phrase "negative to" echoes Fichte's contrast of the ego and the non-ego.

[2] Half of the book had been printed before the second half was written, before its whole conception was clear in Hegel's mind, and before the title "Phenomenology" had occurred to him. Although the preface was written only after the rest of the book was completed, even some of the bound copies of the first edition still include a half title as page 1, immediately after the preface which has Roman numeral page numbers: "First Part. Science of the Experience of Consciousness." This title, to which the sentence in the text alludes, was plainly conceived before Hegel decided on "Phenomenology of the Spirit." Haering, *Hegel*, vol. II, p. 485, notes "that it was only during, or perhaps even after the conclusion of, the printing that Hegel substituted for the previous half title (after the "Preface") . . . another, 'Science of the Phenomenology of the Spirit (without First Part!!)'; yet the latter was substituted only in some copies, and in some in addition to the former and in the wrong place . . ."

[3] Although Baillie here uses "mind," this is one of scores of passages where only "spirit" makes good sense. Cf. II.1, note [27] above. ". . . the spirit is this movement . . ." alludes to the Holy Spirit: God the Father becomes God the Son—he becomes something other for himself, an object for himself—but then this otherhood is canceled and yet preserved in the Holy Spirit. Spirit is that which is not static, nor unstained self-identity; on the contrary, it is of its very essence that it is dynamic, is development, is sublimated otherhood.

[4] The given is experienced as something strange before it becomes, through the experience, the property of consciousness.

and truth is overcome. Being is mediated absolutely; it is substantial content which is just as immediately property of the ego, self-like,[5] or Concept. With this the phenomenology of the spirit is concluded. What the spirit prepares for itself in this phenomenology is the element of knowledge. In this element the moments of the spirit spread themselves out in the form of simplicity which knows its object as itself. They no longer fall apart into the opposition of being and knowledge but abide in the simplicity of knowledge; they are now the true in the form of the true, and their difference is only the difference of content. Their movement which in this element organizes itself into a whole is Logic or speculative philosophy.

11. In what way the Phenomenology of the Spirit is negative or contains what is false[6]

The system of the experience of the spirit deals only with the appearance of the spirit. Hence the progression from this system to the science of the true that also has the form of the true seems to be merely negative. Therefore one might wish to be spared the negative as something false, and one might ask to be led to truth without delay: Why bother with the false?[7]

This demand, mentioned previously, that one should begin straightway with science, one has to answer here by considering quite generally the nature of the negative as something false. The conceptions people have about this are pre-eminent obstacles on the way to truth. This also provides an occasion for speaking of mathematical knowledge which unphilosophical knowledge considers the ideal that philosophy should strive to reach, though so far it has striven in vain.

True and false are among the determinate thoughts which are considered immobile separate essences, as if one stood here and the other there, without community, fixed and isolated. Against this view one must insist that truth is not a minted coin which can be given and pocketed ready-made.[8] Nor does something false exist any more than something evil exists. To be sure, the evil and the false are not as bad as the devil, for in the devil they are even made into a particular

⁵ "self-like": *selbstisch;* a most unusual word.

⁶ Although our division of the preface into twelve sections, following Lasson, does not mark this point, a careful reader would notice that there is a significant break here, even if he did not know that Hegel's original table of contents provided a new heading. This is the end of the first half of the preface, not only in a purely quantitative sense. Hegel has now submitted the major contentions which distinguish his philosophy, and he has explained the purpose of the *Phenomenology* and its relation to his then still unwritten *Logic*.

⁷ Hegel now asks, in effect: Why shouldn't one start straightway with the *Logic* (as English and American students of Hegel have generally done)? In a way Hegel has already answered this question; for example, when he likened the *Phenomenology* to a ladder (II.2, note ⁵ above). Above when Hegel asks, "why bother with the false?" and goes on to say that we must now consider "the nature of the negative as something false," we may feel that this point, too, has long been taken care of; for example, in the fourth paragraph of the preface, where Hegel spoke of bud, blossom, and fruit. But Hegel proposes to return to this question now in order to treat it more systematically and to compare, if only briefly, mathematical, historical, and philosophic truth.

⁸ An allusion to Lessing's play *Nathan der Weise* (1779), the work quoted more often in Hegel's *theologische Jugendschriften*, written in the 1790s, than any other. In Act III, scene 5, Saladin asks Nathan to tell him which of the three religions, Islam, Judaism, and Christianity, is the true one, and to state his reasons. In a soliloquy in scene 6, Nathan exclaims:

> Truth. Truth!
> He wants it so—so ready-made [*so bar, so blank*], as if
> Truth were a coin!—Yes, if at least it were
> A very ancient coin that one must weigh!
> That still might pass. But such a modern coin,
> Made by a stamp, as one may simply lay
> And count upon a board, that it is not.
> Like cash into a bag, truth should be shoved
> Into the head?

In the next scene, when the sultan returns, Nathan tells him the parable of the three rings. (For an English translation see Kaufmann, *The Faith of a Heretic*, section 80.)

subject; as the false and evil they are merely something genera
but still have opposed individual essences.

The false (for only this has a place in our discussion
would be the other, the negative of the substance which, a
the content of knowledge, is the true. But the substance i
itself essentially the negative, partly as the differentiation an
determination of the content, partly as simple discrimina
tion, i.e., as self and knowledge in general. One can knov
something falsely. That something is known falsely mean
that knowledge is not identical with its substance. Yet precisel
this non-identity is differentiation which is an essential mo
ment. Out of this differentiation their identity comes, and thi
resulting identity is the truth. But it is not truth as if non
identity had been thrown away, like dross from pure metal—
nor even as the tool is excluded from the finished vessel
rather non-identity is, as the negative, as the self, still immedi
ately present in the true as such. Yet it does not follow tha
the false may be called a moment of the true, let alone a par
of it. That in everything false there is something true—in thi
dictum both are treated like oil and water which are unmix
able and united only externally. Precisely on account of the
meaning associated with the moment of complete otherhood
such expressions must no longer be used where such other
hood is sublimated. Talk of the unity of subject and object, o
the finite and the infinite, of being and thinking, etc., is mis
leading because object and subject, etc., signify that whic
they are outside their unity, and in the unity they are no
meant in the sense suggested by such an expression. Just so
the false is no longer something false as a moment of truth.

Dogmatism as a style of thought in knowledge and in the
study of philosophy is nothing else than the opinion that the
true consists in a proposition that is a fixed result or that i
known immediately.[9] To such questions as, when Caesar wa
born, or how many feet there were in a stadium, etc., a nea
answer should be given, just as it is surely true that the squar
of the hypotenuse equals the sum of the squares of the othe
two sides of a right-angled triangle. But the nature of sucl
so-called truths is different from the nature of philosophica
truths.

It is indicative of the state of Hegel study in the English-peaking world that one of the most scholarly American his-orians of philosophy has praised Kierkegaard's "indirect pro-est against the Hegelian pretensions to serve up all truth in in objective, cut-and-dried way. He [Kierkegaard] contended strongly that truth is no finished product, which can be handed over the counter of philosophy, quite impersonally and effort-essly" (James Collins, *The Mind of Kierkegaard*, 1953, p. 39). Cf. the following note.

9 Hegel's position is more radical than Kierkegaard's. Kierkegaard accepts some Christian dogmas as propositions that are fixed results and known immediately, to use Hegel's language—or, in Collins' words, he believes that truth "can be handed over the counter of philosophy, quite impersonally and effortlessly." But he insists that the truth of Christianity cannot be *absorbed* impersonally and effortlessly: though it can be *known* immediately, it requires not so much effort as grace to put it into practice, to be changed by it, and to become a Christian in the highest sense of that word. There is nothing particularly radical or novel or anti-Hegelian about this aspect of Kierkegaard's thought; this is traditional Christian preaching. But Hegel insists not merely that it is difficult to put the truth into practice: this he takes for granted and therefore does not stress. But he insists that philosophical truth cannot be *given* in a fixed proposition, like a coin; not only that it cannot be pocketed like that. Philosophical truth is not expressible in formulas that can be learned by heart and recited at pleasure. Cf. I.1, notes 6, 7, 9, 11; I.2, notes 5, 9, 12; II.1, notes 24, 25; II.2, note 1; II.3, notes 4, 6, 28; and note 8 above.

12. Historical and mathematical truth

[III.2]

Regarding historical truths—to mention these briefly—insofar
as their purely historical aspect is considered, it will be readily
granted that they concern particular existence and the accidental and arbitrary side, the features that are not necessary.

But even such bare truths as those adduced here as examples
do not lack the movement of self-consciousness. To know one
of them one must compare much, consult books, or inquire in
some manner; and even where one might appeal to immediate
intuition, such knowledge is held to have true value only when
it is backed up by reasons, although it may be alleged that
only the bare result matters.[2]

As for mathematical truths, it is even more obvious that one
would not consider a man a geometer if he knew Euclid's
theorems by *heart,* but without their proofs—without, as one
might say by way of juxtaposition, also knowing them by
mind.[3] In the same way, if a man by measuring many right-
angled triangles acquired the knowledge that their sides have
the well-known relation to each other, such knowledge would
be considered unsatisfactory. Yet even in mathematical
knowledge, the importance of the demonstration still does not
have the significance and characteristic that it is a moment
of the result itself; in the result the demonstration is over and
has disappeared. As a result, to be sure, the theorem is something whose truth is apprehended. But this additional circum-
stance does not concern its content but only its relation to the
subject; the movement of the mathematical demonstration
does not belong to that which is the object but is an activity
that remains external to the matter. Thus the nature of the
right-angled triangle does not take itself apart after the manner
of the construction that is required for the demonstration of
the proposition that expresses the relations; the whole production of the result is a way and means of knowledge.

In philosophical knowledge, too, the becoming of the exist-

III.2. Historical and mathematical truths

¹ Hegel disposes of historical truths in three sentences. While what he says is remarkably unprofound, he at least makes perfectly plain that the still widely popular notion of Hegel's conception of history is utterly wrong: so far from believing that historical events are necessary and can be deduced *a priori*, Hegel says the very first time he mentions historical truths in his first book that they concern the "accidental and arbitrary." In this respect, he suggests, they differ from philosophical truths.

² Although many teachers in secondary schools believe that research consists in looking up things in an encyclopedia, different encyclopedias frequently disagree even about such "bare truths" as when a great man was born or when a famous book was first published. Any serious student, therefore, must inquire, compare, and support his contentions with reasons. Indeed, one of the "bare truths . . . adduced here as examples" illustrates this point. The traditional date for Caesar's birth was 100 B.C., because Suetonius, Plutarch, and Appian said that he was in his fifty-sixth year when he was assassinated; but Theodor Mommsen, writing a few decades after Hegel's death, convinced most historians that Caesar was born in 102 B.C.

³ The German *auswendig*, literally external, means "by heart"; *inwendig*, which is much less common, means internal and is here used by Hegel for a play on words.

ence as existence is different from the becoming of the essence or inner nature of the matter. But in the first place philosophical knowledge contains both, while mathematical knowledge represents only the becoming of the existence, i.e., the emergence of the nature of the matter in knowledge.[4] Secondly philosophical knowledge also unites these two separate movements. The internal genesis or becoming of the substance is undivided transition into the external or into existence, into being for another; and, conversely, the becoming of existence is a retreat into essence. In this way the movement is the double process and becoming of the whole: each posits the other simultaneously, and therefore each also has both as two aspects of itself. Together they constitute the whole by dissolving themselves and making themselves into its moments.

In mathematical knowledge, insight is an event that is external to the matter; it follows that the true matter is changed by it. The means, construction and demonstration, contain true propositions; but at the same time it must be said that the content is false.[5] In the above example, the triangle is dismembered and its parts are allotted to other figures which the construction brings into being alongside it. Only in the end one reconstitutes the triangle which really matters, but which during the procedure was lost from view and appeared only in pieces which belonged to other wholes.—Here, then, we also see the negativity of the content enter, which would just as much have to be called a falseness of the content as is the disappearance in the movement of the Concept of the thought that had been considered fixed.

The real defectiveness of mathematical knowledge, however, concerns both the knowledge itself and its content.—Regarding the knowledge, the first point is that the necessity of the construction is not apprehended. This does not issue from the Concept of the theorem; rather it is commanded and one must blindly obey the command to draw precisely these lines instead of an indefinite number of others, not because one knows anything but merely in the good faith that this will turn out to be expedient for the conduct of the demonstration. Afterwards this expediency does indeed become manifest, but it is an external expediency because it manifests itself only after the demonstration.[6]

⁴ Hegel claims that mathematical demonstrations, at least of the kind he discusses, involve an epistemological process only, not also an ontological one, while in philosophy the two are inseparable. His terminology and his way of putting the point, so far from increasing precision and clarity, create wholly unnecessary difficulties. Hegel says—to translate the end of his sentence just a little more literally than we have done in the text: "But in the first place the philosophical knowledge contains both, while the mathematical represents only the becoming of the existence [*Dasein*], i.e., of the being of the nature of the matter in knowledge as such." The point is surely that in mathematical demonstrations, according to Hegel, we witness the development of knowledge about something, but not the development of that which is known: the demonstration remains external to the content of knowledge. And because it remains external to the content, it may be said that it does not penetrate the essence of, say, a triangle. But when Hegel distinguishes essence and existence (in the immediately preceding sentence he contrasts *Dasein* and *Wesen* most emphatically) and then goes on to say that mathematical demonstrations represent "only the becoming of the existence," he surely makes things unnecessarily difficult and confusing for the reader.

⁵ This is a rather impressionistic use of the word "false" (*falsch*).

⁶ Hermann Glockner, *Hegel*, vol. II (1940), p. 455, says: "I do not wish to inquire here whether Hegel's account holds up; I only wish to point out that his critique coincides, down to the details of the chosen example, with that of his later antipode, Arthur Schopenhauer." A footnote refers us to *The World as Will and Idea*, I, § 15, and remarks that "there are several parallel passages," before Glockner proceeds: "Yet Hegel's critique of mathematical method differs from Schopenhauer's in one very significant respect. While the latter insists above all on 'pure intuition' and 'analytical method,' Hegel tries to make clear the one-sidedness or defectiveness of mathematical concept formation. . . ."

Here is a translation of parts of Schopenhauer's long § 15: We are convinced that intuition is the primary source of all evidence, and the immediate or mediated reference to it alone is absolute truth, and that the nearest way to it is always the safest because every mediation through Concepts exposes us to many deceptions. When with this conviction we turn to mathematics, as it was set up as a science by Euclid and has

Just so, the demonstration follows a path that begins som
where—one does not yet know in what relation to the resu
that is to be attained. As it proceeds, these determinations ar
relations are taken up while others are ignored, although on
does not by any means see immediately according to wh
necessity. An external purpose rules this movement.

The evident certainty of this defective knowledge, of whic
mathematics is proud and of which it also boasts as again
philosophy, rests solely on the poverty of its purpose and tl
defectiveness of its material and is therefore of a kind th
philosophy must spurn.—Its purpose or Concept is magnitud
This is precisely the relation that is not essential and is void of
Concept.[7] The movement of knowledge therefore proceeds c
the surface, does not touch the matter itself, not the essenc
or the Concept, and is therefore not comprehension.

The material about which mathematics offers such a plea
ing treasure of truths is space and the unit. Space is tl
existence into which the Concept writes its distinctions as in
an empty, dead element in which they are equally immobi
and lifeless. The actual is not something spatial the way it
considered in mathematics; with such unactuality as is exen
plified by the things of mathematics neither concrete sen
intuition nor philosophy concerns itself. In such an unactu
element there are only unactual truths, i.e., fixed, dead prop
sitions: one can stop with any one of them; the following on
starts anew for itself, and the first one does not move itse
on to the next, nor does a necessary connection come abo
in this way through the nature of the matter.—Also, on accou
of this principle and element—and in this consists the forma
ism of the evident certainty of mathematics—knowledge pro
ceeds along the line of equality. For what is dead and do
not move itself does not attain the differentiation of its essenc
or the essential opposition and inequality; and therefore
also does not attain the transition from the opposed into tl
opposed, nor the qualitative, immanent movement, nor se
movement. For mathematics considers only magnitude whic

n the whole remained to this day, we cannot help finding the
ay it pursues strange—indeed, perverted [*verkehrt*] . . . in-
tead of thus granting a thorough insight into the essence of
ie triangle, he sets up a few disjointed, arbitrarily chosen
ropositions about the triangle and offers a logical reason for
iem by way of a tortuous, logical proof. . . . Instead of an
xhaustive knowledge of these spatial relations, one therefore
eceives merely a few . . . results from them and is in the
osition of a person to whom the various effects of a complex
iachine are shown, while their inner relation and the works
re kept from him. That what Euclid demonstrates is indeed
iat way, one has to admit, compelled by the principle of
ontradiction: but *why* things are that way, one is not told.
)ne therefore has almost the uncomfortable feeling that at-
ends a sleight of hand; and in fact most Euclidean proofs are
trikingly similar to that. Almost always truth enters through
ie backdoor. . . . Often, as in the Pythagorean theorem,
nes are drawn, one knows not why: afterwards it appears
iat they were nooses that are unexpectedly tightened and
aptivate the assent of the student who now has to admit,
mazed, what in its inner context remains totally incompre-
ensible for him—so much so that he can study all of Euclid
/ithout gaining any insight into the laws of spatial relations;
istead he would merely learn by heart a few of their results.
'his really empirical and unscientific knowledge is like that
f a doctor who knows disease and remedy, but not their con-
ection. . . . Just so, the Pythagorean theorem teaches us to
now a *qualitas occulta* of the right-angled triangle: Euclid's
tilted, really crafty proof leaves us when it comes to the why,
nd the accompanying familiar simple figure offers at a single
lance far more insight into the matter . . . than that proof:

n the case of unequal sides, too, it must be possible to
chieve such intuitive conviction; indeed this must be so in
ie case of every possible geometrical truth if only because its
iscovery always was prompted by such an intuitive necessity
nd the proof was thought out only afterwards . . ."

§ 15 comprises almost twenty pages; our quotations come

is the unessential difference.[7] Mathematics abstracts from 1 fact that it is the Concept that bifurcates[8] space into its dim sions and determines the relations of and in these. It dc not consider, e.g., the relation of the line to the plane; a when it compares the diameter of the circle with the circu ference it comes up against incommensurability, i.e., a re tion of the Concept, something infinite that escapes matl matical determination.

Immanent or so-called pure mathematics also does not ju tapose time as time with space, as the second material for consideration. Applied mathematics, to be sure, does treat it as well as of movement and other actual things. But it tak the synthetic propositions, i.e., those about their relatio which are determined by their Concept, from experience, a it merely applies its formulas to these assumptions. The s called demonstrations of such propositions as those abc the equilibrium of the lever, or the relation of space and ti in the movement of a fall, etc., are often given and accept as demonstrations; but this only demonstrates how great need knowledge has of demonstrations: where it lacks ar thing more, it respects even the empty semblance of a demo stration and thus gains some satisfaction. A critique of the demonstrations[9] would be as remarkable as it would be i structive and might both cleanse mathematics of this fa finery and show the limitations of mathematics and thus al the necessity of another kind of knowledge.

As for time, of which one should think that, juxtapos with space, it would constitute the material of the other pa of pure mathematics, it is the existing Concept itself.[10] T principle of magnitude, that difference void of Concept, a the principle of equality, that abstract and lifeless unity, a incapable of concerning themselves with this pure unrest life and this absolute differentiation. This negativity, ther fore, becomes the second material for this knowledge only paralyzed form, namely as the unit; and this knowledge, b ing external to its content, reduces that which moves itself mere material in which it then has an indifferent, extern lifeless content.

from the first quarter, and some of our omissions are considerable. Extremely long sentences have been broken up in translation, no less than in Hegel's text. Schopenhauer, born February 22, 1788, was barely nineteen when the *Phenomenology* appeared in 1807. By the time *The World as Will and Idea* was published in 1819, he was very much aware of Hegel's philosophy, and until his death in 1860 he never tired of heaping outright abuse on Hegel in print. For his encounter with Hegel at Berlin, see H 54.

[7] Quantitative differences, as opposed to qualitative ones, do not concern the essence of a thing: as soon as they do, we say that the difference is not merely quantitative.

[8] Since space is usually taken to have three dimensions, "bifurcates" is a little odd; but Hegel says *entzweit*.

[9] Lasson says in a footnote: "In the *Encyclopedia*, § 267, Hegel illuminated the laws of gravitation more closely in this sense."

[10] That time is the existing Concept itself (*der daseiende Begriff selbst*) is here thrown out *en passant* as an epigram split in two by a parenthesis twice as long as the epigram itself. Perhaps one should recall Plato's remark in the *Timaeus* (37) that time is "a moving image of eternity." Plato first introduces this haunting phrase and then says, a few lines later: "and this image we call time." For Hegel, time is not an image of the Concept but the existing Concept itself. The Concept, as we have seen (especially in II.3, note [37]), is fluid by nature—it is of its very essence that it transcends fixity—and its existence, the existence of such fluidity, involves time. But the *obiter dictum* that time *is* "the existing Concept itself" illustrates Hegel's esprit rather better than "the elevation of philosophy to a science" (I.1, text for note [13]).

13. The nature of philosophical truth and its method

[III.3]

Philosophy, on the other hand, considers not the inessenti[al] determination but the determination insofar as it is essential. Not the abstract or unactual is its element and contents b[ut] the actual, that which posits itself and lives in itself, existen[t] in its Concept.[2] It is the process that generates and ru[ns] through its moments, and this whole movement constitutes th[e] positive and its truth. This truth, then, includes the negati[ve] as well—that which might be called the false if it could [be] considered as something from which one should abstract. Th[e] evanescent must, however, be considered essential—not in th[e] determination of something fixed that is to be severed fro[m] the true and left lying outside it, one does not know wher[e,] nor does the true rest on the other side, dead and positiv[e.] The appearance is the coming to be and passing away th[at] itself does not come to be or pass away; it is in itself an[d] constitutes the actuality and the movement of the life of th[e] truth.[3] The true is thus the bacchanalian whirl in which n[o] member is not drunken; and because each, as soon as it de[-] taches itself, dissolves immediately—the whirl is just as muc[h] transparent and simple repose.[4] In the court of justice of th[is] movement, to be sure, the individual forms of the spirit endu[re] no more than determinate thoughts do, yet they are just a[s] much positive and necessary moments as they are negativ[e] and evanescent.—In the whole of the movement, considerin[g] it as repose, that which distinguishes itself in it and gives pa[r-] ticular existence is preserved as something that remember[s]

III.3. Philosophical truth

¹ In the first paragraph of III.2 we were told that historical truth is concerned with the accidental and arbitrary; for example, when Caesar was born. In the longer discussion of mathematical truths Hegel tried to show in various ways that the geometer does not reach the essence of the triangle, for example. Philosophy, on the other hand, concerns itself with the essence of what it studies. An example may help. While the historian of art or religion must occupy himself with accidental events that were not necessary, the philosopher of art or religion must ask about the essence of art or religion.

² When Hegel insists that the philosopher is concerned with the essence, he does not by any means concede that existence is of no concern to him. Any dichotomy of that sort between essence and existence would strike him as utterly subphilosophical. As he uses these terms, mathematics, so far from dealing with essences, deals with the abstract or unactual; and philosophy, which deals with what is essential, deals necessarily with the actual.

³ The evanescent is essential: for this and what follows we have been prepared in the opening paragraphs of the preface in which Hegel eventually disparaged "the naked result."

⁴ This very striking sentence is one of the most memorable and famous Hegel ever wrote. It is doubly noteworthy that, as published by him in 1807, it cannot be construed. And though he made dozens of changes, mostly minute, in the early pages of the preface, he evidently never noticed that this flamboyant dictum sorely needed another pronoun to make sense; at least he left no notation to indicate which pronoun should be inserted. The first half sentence is inelegant enough with its double negative; the second half reads in the first edition: *und weil jedes, indem es sich absondert, ebenso unmittelbar auflöst,—ist er ebenso die durchsichtige und einfache Ruhe.* But *auflösen*, unlike "dissolve," is never intransitive. In the posthumous edition of 1832, the editor inserted *sich* before *auflöst:* "and because each, as it detaches itself, just as immediately dissolves (*itself*) . . ." Lasson, on the

and its existence is knowledge of itself even as this knowledge is just as immediately existence.[5]

It might seem necessary to devote a lengthy preamble to the method of this movement or of science. But the Concept of this method is implicit in what has been said, and its real exposition belongs to the Logic, or rather constitutes the Logic. For the method is nothing else than the edifice of the whole, constructed in its pure essence. But the entire system of prevalent notions of philosophical method belongs to a extinct form of education.

If this should sound boastful or revolutionary, though know that my tone is altogether different, it should be noted that the scientific finery furnished by mathematics—such as explanations, divisions, axioms, rows of theorems, their demonstrations, principles, and deductions and inferences from them—is at least according to current opinion quite outmoded. Even if the unfitness of these procedures is not yet clearly understood, one makes little or no use of them; and if one does not disapprove of them, at least they are not loved. And we must have the prejudice in favor of what is excellent that it will get itself used[6] and loved.

But it is not difficult to see that positing a proposition, adducing reasons for it, and in the same way refuting the opposite by giving reasons, cannot be the form in which truth appears. Truth is its own self-movement, while this is the method of knowledge that remains external to its material. It is peculiar to, and must be left to, mathematics which, as we have noted, has for its principle the relation of magnitude—a relation void of Concept—and for its material dead space and the equally dead unit. In a somewhat freer style, i.e., mixed more with the arbitrary and the accidental, this method may retain its place in ordinary life, in conversation, or in historical instruction which is aimed at curiosity more than at knowl-

other hand, thought it made more sense to suppose that *er* had dropped out after *weil:* "because it (the whirl) dissolves each . . ." Hoffmeister went back to the reading of 1832; so do I. The difference in meaning seems negligible: what is interesting is the fact that Hegel himself did not do anything about this flaw in one of his most colorful and oft quoted sentences.

Royce knew enough German to be able, when he misquoted this dictum in his *Lectures on Modern Idealism*, 215 f., to do so in fluent German as well as English: "As Hegel boldly expressed the situation, in the metaphorical language of his early period, and of his *Phaenomenologie,* 'The truth is the Bacchanalian revel, wherein every one of the finite forms of the truth appears as an intoxicated illusion.' (*Die Wahrheit ist der Bacchantische Taumel, worin alle Gestalten trunken sind.*)" This is entirely characteristic of Royce's excessively free interpretation of Hegel (cf. H 29)—and of J. Loewenberg's editing (cf. H 52, n. [5]). Royce's *Lectures* were published posthumously, and Loewenberg said in his "Editor's Preface": "Written as they were for oral delivery the lectures required much revision; the editor hopes he has not used his pen too freely." One wonders why he did not catch this mistranslation and misquotation: after all, the reference to "illusion," of which there is no trace in Hegel, is as characteristic of Anglo-American Idealism as it is alien to the whole spirit of Hegel's work. But Loewenberg also failed to correct Royce's wrong dates, e.g., on pp. 101 and 142.

What Hegel means is plainly that the forms of consciousness that are examined in the *Phenomenology* are all unbalanced and a little ridiculous; they exist and can be illustrated from history; but they are evanescent—passing stages in the story of the spirit's *Bildung;* and as we recall that story and behold them all at once or singly—detached—as we turn the pages of the book, the whirl has lost its fury and appears as tranquil repose. Indeed, the second half-sentence, about dissolution and repose, is bound to be more obvious to Hegel's readers than the first. What requires emphasis is that he himself did not merely recollect in tranquillity but also had a sense of the Dionysian whirl.

[5] An allusion to the end of the *Phenomenology*.

[6] A polemical allusion to the last sentence of Spinoza's *Ethics:* "But everything excellent is as difficult as it is rare." Hegel has the faith that what is excellent prevails and gains currency—*dass es sich in den Gebrauch setze*.

edge—and therefore perhaps also in a preface.[7] In ordinary
life, consciousness has for its contents information, experiences, sense concretions, also thoughts, principles—altogether
what is considered as a datum or as a being or essence in fixed
repose. Now consciousness follows this thread, now it interrupts the connection by freely and arbitrarily disposing of
such contents, and altogether consciousness here treats and
determines its contents from the outside. Things are led back
to some certainty, even if that is only the feeling of the moment; and conviction is satisfied when it has reached a familiar
point of rest.

While the necessity of the Concept banishes the looser gait
of conversational arguments as well as the stiffer gait of scientific pomp, it has been pointed out above that their place must
not be taken by the unmethod of intimation[8] and enthusiasm
and the arbitrariness of prophetic speech which despises not
only this scientific pomp but scientific procedures quite generally.

14. Against schematizing formalism

Now that Kant, by instinct, has rediscovered triplicity, albeit still dead and still uncomprehended, and it has subsequently been raised to its absolute importance, and with it
the true form in its true content has been presented and the
Concept of science has emerged, it is equally obvious that we
must not consider scientific that use of this form which reduces it to a lifeless schema,[9] really to a phantom,[10] and
scientific organization to a table.[11]

In a general way this formalism has already been discussed
above, but we now want to describe its manner in a little more
detail. This formalism supposes it has comprehended and expressed the nature and life of a form when it merely ascribes
to it as a predicate some determination of the schema; e.g.
subjectivity or objectivity, or magnetism, electricity, etc., contraction or expansion, east or west, et al. This sort of thing can
be multiplied ad infinitum because in this manner every determination or form can be used again as a form or moment
of the schema when it comes to another, and each can grate

[7] As in I.1.4 above, Hegel casts aspersions on his own preface.

[8] *Ahndung:* an allusion to Jakob Friedrich Fries, *Wissen, Glaube und Ahndung* (Knowledge, Faith, and Intimation), Jena, 1805. Fries, Hegel's contemporary at Jena, had become Professor of Philosophy at Heidelberg in 1806. When he accepted a chair at Jena in 1816, Hegel became his successor at Heidelberg.

In the twentieth century, Leonard Nelson founded a Neo-Friesian School. The conception of *Ahnung* (*Ahndung* is now wholly obsolete) was also revived by Rudolf Otto in his classic, *Das Heilige* (1917). In the English version, *The Idea of the Holy* (1923; often reprinted), *Ahnung* is rendered somewhat oddly as "divination."

[9] *Schema.*

[10] *Schemen.* The pun is lost in translation.

[11] Kant's rediscovery of triplicity: After offering his table of twelve categories in the *Critique of Pure Reason,* Kant added some remarks in the second edition (1787): "About this table of categories one can offer some neat observations [*artige Betrachtungen*] which might well have considerable consequences in regard to the scientific form of all knowledge of reason. . . . 2d Note: That everywhere the number of the categories in each class is the same, namely three, which also calls for reflection since elsewhere all division *a priori* by means of Concepts must be dichotomy. And on top of that [*Dazu kommt aber noch, dass*] the third category always emerges from the connection of the second with the first of its class. Thus totality is nothing else than plurality considered as unity; limitation nothing else than reality connected with negation; community is the causality of a substance in the determination of another, reciprocally; finally, necessity nothing else than the existence that is given by the possibility itself. . . ." (B 109–11; cf. *Prolegomena,* 1783, § 39, footnote.)

Hegel speaks of a rediscovery because this sort of triplicity had played a great role in Neoplatonism, especially in Proclus (412–85). It was again raised to "absolute importance" by Fichte who made much of theses, antitheses, and syntheses. Glockner suggests that Hegel here means to lump Schelling with Fichte, including him in his encomium: "The few words in which Hegel expresses this high praise of Fichte and Schelling almost in passing are remarkable. For they show that the

fully perform the same service for another. But in this circle of reciprocity one never learns what the matter itself is—neither what the one nor what the other is. In this process one sometimes uses sense determinations from common intuition—but then these are supposed to mean something different from what they say—and sometimes one uses the pure determinations of thoughts, meaningful in themselves, such as subject, object, substance, cause, the general, etc.—but just as uncritically and without examination as in ordinary life and as strengths and weaknesses, expansion and contraction. This metaphysics, then, is as unscientific as these sense conceptions

Instead of the inner life and the self-movement of its existence, such a simple determinateness is taken from intuition which here means the knowledge of the senses, and expressed according to a superficial analogy, and then this external and empty application of a formula is called construction.—Such formalism is like any other. How dull would a mind have to be that could not learn in a quarter of an hour the theory that there are asthenic, sthenic, and indirectly asthenic diseases and equally many attempts at cures! And since such instruction was until quite recently considered sufficient, anybody but a dullard could in such a short span of time be transformed from a *routinier* into a theoretical physician.[12] The formalism of such philosophy of nature teaches, say, that the understanding is electricity, or that animals are nitrogen or equal the south or north, etc., or represent it—whether all this is expressed as nakedly as here or brewed up with a little more terminology. Confronted with such power that brings together what had seemed far apart, and with the violence that the calmly restful things of sense suffer from such connections while they thus receive the semblance of a Concept, though they are spared the main thing, namely to express the Concept itself or the significance of the notion of the senses—confronted with all this, inexperience may well be plunged into admiration and amazement, and it may even venerate in all this the signs of profound genius. Inexperience may also be delighted by the good cheer of such determinations, since they substitute something that can be intuited for the abstract Concept and thus make things more pleasing, and inexperience

immediately following sharp attack on romantic philosophy of nature was indeed meant to be directed only against its excrescences but not against Schelling himself" (II, 460; a footnote refers to Hegel's letter to Schelling, May 1, 1807, but not to Schelling's reply: see D 1807 for both).

Another interpretation would reserve the praise for Fichte and the critique for Schelling. In that case, to be sure, Hegel's letter to Schelling was simply dishonest. But Hegel was not thinking so much in terms of personalities, and what he meant was almost certainly: After Kant, the triplicity on which he had remarked in passing and whose importance he suspected without comprehending it, was raised to absolute importance, first of all, but by no means only, in Fichte's *Doctrine of Science (Wissenschaftslehre)* in 1794. Schelling, too, shared in the development of this great insight. But both also reduced triplicity to a lifeless schema. The detailed attack that follows could hardly be directed only against Schelling's imitators. The point might be put best by saying that, as Hegel saw it, Schelling himself had not always retained the *niveau* of his own greatest contributions to philosophy: again and again he had fallen to the level of a mere Schellingian. See H 39.

What is much more interesting and important than these historical considerations, however, is that Hegel once again goes out of his way to attack the very views which posterity, ironically, came to associate with him. Ever since the mid-nineteenth century, Hegel himself has been ridiculed for allegedly holding the views which he mocks here.

may even congratulate itself on its intimation of an affinity of souls with such glorious activity.[12]

The trick of such wisdom is learned as quickly as it is easy to master it; its repetition, once it is known, becomes as insufferable as the repetition of a sleight of hand one sees through. The instrument of this monotonous formalism is no more difficult to handle than a painter's palette on which there are only two colors, say, red and green, one if an historical piece is wanted, the other for landscapes.[13]

It would be difficult to decide what is greater—the smugness with which everything in the heavens, on earth, and beneath the earth is coated with such a broth of paint, or the conceit that is based on the supposed excellence of this panacea: each supports the other.[14] The product of this method of labeling everything in heaven and earth, all natural and spiritual forms, with a few determinations of the general schema, and thus pigeonholing everything, is nothing less than a sun-clear report[15] on the organism of the universe—namely a tabulation that is like a skeleton with little pieces of paper stuck all over it, or like the rows of closed, labeled jars in a spicer's stall. While it is as explicit as both of these, it is like them in other ways too: here, flesh and blood are removed from the bones; there, the also not living matter is concealed in jars; and in the report, the living essence of the matter is left out.[16]

This manner has been further perfected into monochromatic absolute painting: ashamed of the distinctions of the schema, one drowns them in the emptiness of the absolute because they belong to reflection, and the new product is then pure identity, formless white.[17] But this has been noted above. That monotony of the schema and its lifeless determinations and this absolute identity, and the transition from one to the other—all are equally dead understanding and equally external knowledge.

The excellent, however, not only cannot escape the fate of being thus deprived of life and spirit, of being flayed and then seeing its skin wrapped around lifeless knowledge and its vanity. Rather we can recognize even in this fate the power of the excellent over the hearts, even if not over minds; also the development toward the generality and determinateness of

¹² Hegel's long sentences have been broken up throughout. In that respect our translation is not faithful to the style of the original. By way of compensation, a few long sentences are indicated in this commentary; for example, the passage that runs from here to the end of this paragraph ("The formalism of such . . . glorious activity") forms a single sentence in the original.

¹³ At its best—here, for example—Hegel's ridicule is easily as good as Kierkegaard's at its best.

¹⁴ The passage from this point to the end of this paragraph ("The product . . . is left out") forms a single sentence in the original.

¹⁵ This phrase alludes to Fichte's *Sun-clear Report to the Public at Large* . . . (see I.1, note ¹³ above). This mocking allusion helps to confirm our suggestion that Fichte as well as Schelling had been guilty, according to Hegel, of reducing triplicity to a lifeless schema.

¹⁶ One should here recall Mephistopheles' remarks about *Collegium Logicum* in *Faust* I, lines 1911–41. Hegel knew this scene as it had been included in *Faust: A Fragment* (1790). Readers of *Faust* who have been gulled by the Hegel legend have often associated this passage with Hegel (who was twenty in 1790). Actually, this scene was already part of the *Urfaust,* written before 1775, before Schelling was even born and before Fichte was thirteen and Hegel five.

> Days will be spent to let you know
> That what you once did at one blow,
> Like eating and drinking so easy and free,
> Can only be done with One, Two, Three. . . .
> The philosopher comes with analysis
> And proves it had to be like this:
> The first was so, the second so,
> And hence the third and fourth was so,
> And were not the first and the second here,
> Then the third and fourth could never appear. . . .
> Who would study and describe the living, starts
> By driving the spirit out of the parts:
> In the palm of his hand he holds all the sections,
> Lacks nothing, except the spirit's connections. . . .

¹⁷ This is surely an allusion to Schelling, and it harks back to the jibe about the night in which all cows are black, at the end of section I.3. Some relevant quotations from Schelling were adduced there, in note ¹⁹.

the form which constitutes its perfection and which alone makes it possible that this generality can be used in the service of superficiality.

Science may organize itself only through the life of the Concept; the determinateness which some would take externally from the schema to affix it to existence is in science the self-moving soul of the abundant content. The movement of beings is, first,[18] to become something other and thus to become their own immanent content; secondly,[19] they take back into themselves this unfolding or this existence of theirs, i.e., they make themselves into a mere moment and simplify themselves into determinateness. In the first[20] movement negativity consists in the differentiation and positing of existence; in the return into oneself it is the becoming of determinate simplicity. In this way, the content does not receive its determinateness from another, like a label; instead it determines itself and assigns itself its place as a moment of the whole. The tabular understanding keeps to itself the necessity and the Concept of the contents—that which constitutes the concreteness, the actuality, and the living movement of the matter that it arranges— or rather, the tabular understanding does not keep this to itself, it does not know this; for if it had this insight it would surely show it. It does not even know the need for it; otherwise it would stop schematizing, or at least know that this process produces no more than a table of contents: it gives only the table of contents; the content itself, however, it does not furnish.

Suppose even that the determinateness is, like magnetism, e.g., concrete in itself and actual: even then it is reduced to something dead, as it is merely predicated of some other existence instead of being known as the immanent life of this existence, or as that which has its native and characteristic self-generation and presentation in this existence. The formal understanding leaves it to others to add this main point.

Instead of entering into the immanent content of the matter, it always looks over[21] the whole and stands above the individual existence of which it speaks, i.e., it simply overlooks it.[22] Scientific knowledge, however, demands precisely that we surrender to the life of the object or—and this is the same— that we confront and express its inner necessity.[23] Thus im-

[18] "first": *einesteils;* more literally: on the one hand.

[19] "secondly": *anderenteils* or on the other hand.

[20] *In jener Bewegung:* in that movement. Glockner summarizes this sentence and the preceding one by saying: "Hegel describes the three-step: thesis, antithesis, synthesis" (II, 460). But according to Glockner's own four-volume *Hegel-Lexikon* (a very elaborate and helpful index to his twenty-volume *Jubiläumsausgabe* of Hegel's works), thesis, antithesis, and synthesis are only once mentioned together by Hegel—disparagingly, in his lectures on the history of philosophy, toward the end of his critique of Kant. (Cf. WK 166–67, and Gustav E. Mueller's "The Hegel Legend of 'Thesis-Antithesis-Synthesis.' ")

[21] "looks over": *übersieht.* The German word can mean both survey and also overlook in the sense of not seeing. The first meaning is intended here.

[22] "overlooks it": *sieht es gar nicht.* This can only mean: does not see it at all. I have tried to keep the pun in English.

[23] This harks back to I.1.8 above. At this point Hegel's conception of the ethos of scientific work is by no means remote from positivism or from Max Weber's classical statement in *Wissenschaft als Beruf* (1919; Scholarship as a Vocation). Hegel's influence may even have contributed to the fact that in 1919 *Wissenschaft* could still be used in this broad sense for scholarly work in general; and Weber, though far from being a Hegelian, was close to Hegel's spirit when he said: " 'Personality' in the area of scholarship is restricted to those who serve exclusively the subject [*rein der Sache*]" (p. 13). What matters to Hegel is that the impetus that leads from point to point should not come from the arbitrary disposition of the writer but rather from the subject matter. A thorough analysis of one Concept, for example, should require that the analysis proceed to a second Concept, and in this way we should be led on and on by the "inner necessity" of the content. If the analysis should concentrate on the whole position, as it does in the *Phenomenology,* i.e., on the form of consciousness as well as the content, then we should still immerse ourselves in each position in turn, taking it more seriously than its actual proponents, and find that, thus pushed to its limits, it gives way to another position which must then be considered next.

mersed in its object, scientific knowledge forgets that survey which is merely the reflection of knowledge out of the content into itself. But absorbed in the matter and following the movement of that, it returns to itself—but not until the abundance of the content, simplified into determinateness, returns into itself, reduces itself to one side of existence, and develops into its higher truth. Thus the simple whole that surveys itself emerges from the riches in which its reflection had seemed lost.

Because, as we put it above, the substance is in itself subject, all content is its own reflection in itself.[24] The subsistence or substance of an existence is self-identity; for its non-identity with itself would be its dissolution. But self-identity is pure abstraction; but this is thinking.[25] When I say quality, I say simple determinateness. By its quality an existence is different from another, or is existence; it is for itself, or it subsists through this simplicity with itself. But through this it is essentially thought.—In this the fact is comprehended that being is thinking; and this includes the insight that eludes the usual talk, void of Concept, of the identity of thinking and being.[26]

Inasmuch as the subsistence of existence is self-identity or pure abstraction, it is its own abstraction from itself, or it is itself its non-identity with itself and its dissolution—its own inwardness and return into itself—its becoming.[27] Insofar as this is the nature of beings, and beings have this nature for knowledge, knowledge is not an activity that handles its content as something strange—not reflection into itself, away from the content. Science is not that idealism that replaced the dogmatism of assertions with a dogmatism of assurances or a dogmatism of self-certainty. Rather, when knowledge sees the content return into its own inwardness, the activity of knowledge is both absorbed in the content, being its immanent self, and at the same time this knowledge has returned into itself, for it is pure self-identity in otherness. Thus it is the cunning[28] that seems to abstain from activity while it looks on as determinateness and its concrete life suppose that they are pursuing their self-preservation and particular interests though in fact they are the converse, an activity that dissolves itself and makes itself a moment of the whole.

²⁴ "In the following sentences," says Glockner (II, 461), "Hegel accomplishes the decisive, and as I see it extraordinarily problematic, *turn to Panlogism*." This is Glockner's coinage, and what he means by *Panlogismus* is similar to what is more often called rationalism. See the next note.

²⁵ After the sentence cited in the previous note, Glockner quotes the two sentences between our ²⁴ and ²⁵ and comments: "It should be remarked that 'identity' is certainly a logical determination; yet it won't do to conceive something existing and self-identical as for that reason essentially 'thought-ful' ['*gedanklich*']. In that case one leaves out of consideration the moments of individual singularity and organic wholeness, or one logicizes them; i.e., one works merely with positing and opposition, position and negation."

²⁶ The third fragment of Parmenides of Elea (born about 510 B.C.) has often been interpreted as saying: "thinking and being are the same thing." Twentieth-century philologists have offered many other translations.

²⁷ The passage from here to the end of the paragraph forms a single sentence in the original.

²⁸ "the cunning": *die List*. This conception was later developed by Hegel and called *die List der Vernunft* (the cunning of reason): first, in his *Encyclopedia* (1817, § 158; 3d edition, 1830, § 209) and then in a famous passage in his introductory lectures on the philosophy of history: "The particular has its own interest in world history; it is something finite and as such must perish. It is the particular that wearies itself fighting against each other and a part of which is ruined. But precisely in the fight, in the destruction of the particular, the universal results. This is not disturbed. It is not the universal idea that incurs opposition and fight and danger: it keeps itself safe from attack and unharmed in the background, while sending the particular of passion into the fight to wear itself out. One can call it the cunning of reason that it lets the passions do its work, while that through which it translates itself into existence loses and suffers harm. . . . The individuals are sacrificed and surrendered. The idea pays the tribute of existence and transitoriness not out of itself but through the passions of individuals" (VG 105 L). Cf. H 62.

Above, we indicated the significance of the understanding with reference to the self-consciousness of substance; from what has now been said one can see its significance with reference to the determination of substance as having being. Existence is quality, self-identical determinateness or determinate simplicity, determinate thought; this is the understanding of existence. Thus it is *nous,* as Anaxagoras[29] was the first to recognize. Those who came after him comprehended the nature of existence more determinately as *eidos* or *idea,*[30] i.e., determinate generality, species. The expression "species" may seem too common and inferior for the Ideas, for the beautiful, holy, and eternal which are now in fashion. But in fact the Idea expresses no more, nor less, than the species. Yet in our day an expression that designates a Concept precisely is often spurned in favor of another term which, if only because it belongs to a foreign language, shrouds the Concept in a fog and thus sounds more edifying.

Precisely when existence is determined as species it is simple thought; the *nous,* the simplicity, is the substance. On account of its simplicity or self-identity it appears firm and enduring. But this self-identity is also negativity; therefore this firm existence passes over into its dissolution. The determinateness at first seems merely due to the fact that it is related to something else, and the movement seems imposed on it by an alien power; but what is contained in this simplicity of thinking is precisely that this determinateness is qualified by its own otherhood and is thus self-movement. For it is the thought that moves and differentiates itself, its own inwardness, the pure Concept. Thus reasonableness is a becoming, and as such becoming it is rationality.

In this nature of beings, to be their Concept in their being,[31] consists logical necessity. This alone is the rational and the rhythm of the organic whole; it is just as much the knowledge of the content as the content is Concept and essence—or it alone is what is speculative.

The concrete form, moving itself, makes itself into simple determinateness. Thus it raises itself to become logical form and attain its essential nature. Its concrete existence is nothing but this movement and is immediately logical existence. There-

[29] The only other proper names mentioned so far in the preface are Aristotle's and Kant's; toward the end, Plato is mentioned, too. The reference to Anaxagoras (about 500–428/7) harks back to Aristotle's *Metaphysics* (A, end of 3, 984b): when Anaxagoras said "that reason was present—as in animals, so throughout nature—as the cause of order and of all arrangement, he seemed like a sober man in contrast with the random talk of his predecessors" (the W. D. Ross translation; *nous* is the Greek word he translated as reason).

[30] The reference here is to Plato.

[31] This clause sounds even far worse in German: *in seinem Sein sein Begriff zu sein.* Hegel's claim that "logical necessity . . . alone is . . . rational" seems highly implausible and objectionable. See I.1, note [6] above. What Hegel is driving at is explained to some extent in note [23] above.

fore it is unnecessary to impose formalism externally on the concrete content: the content is in itself the transition into formalism which, however, ceases to be this external formalism because the form is the native development of the concrete content itself.

This nature of the scientific method—to be partly not separate from the content, and partly to determine its rhythm by itself—receives, as already mentioned, its proper exposition in speculative philosophy.[32]

What has here been said, to be sure, expresses the Concept, but cannot count for more than an anticipatory assurance. Its truth does not lie in this partly narrative exposition; therefore it also cannot be refuted by the opposed assurance that things are not so but otherwise, or by recalling and recounting conventional conceptions as if they were established and familiar truths, or by assurances of something newly dished up from the shrine of inward divine intuition.

A reception of this sort is usually the first reaction of knowledge to something unfamiliar: one wants to save one's freedom and one's own insight and authority from the alien one—for that which is now first encountered appears in this form. Also, one wants to remove the appearance, and the sort of shame that is supposed to lie in this, that something has been learned. Similarly, when the unfamiliar is accepted with applause, the reaction is motivated the same way and consists in what in another sphere would take the form of ultra-revolutionary speech and action.

[32] "speculative philosophy": Hegel's then still unwritten *Logic* is meant.

At this point there is another sudden shift in tone: the style becomes once again concrete, even earthy.

The final paragraph of this section (beginning "A reception of this sort . . .") seems close to Nietzsche and psychoanalysis. Here Hegel tries to uncover the hidden motives that underlie men's reactions to a new doctrine: one feels in danger of being overpowered and prepares to meet a form of aggression. Hegel suggests that even applause is an outlet for aggressive impulses—a kind of counterattack.

15. The demands of the study of philosophy

[IV.1]

What therefore matters in the study of science is taking upon oneself the exertion of the Concept.[1] What is wanted is attention to the Concept as such, to the simple determinations e.g., of being in itself, being for itself, self-identity, etc.; for these are such pure self-movements which one might call souls if their Concept did not designate something higher. To those accustomed to progress from notion to notion, being interrupted by the Concept seems just as bothersome as it does to formalistic thinking that argues back and forth in unactual thoughts.[3] The former custom should be called material thinking—an accidental consciousness that is merely absorbed in the material and therefore finds it hard to lift the self at the same time clear out of the material to be with itself.[4] The other type, argumentative thinking,[5] is, on the contrary, the freedom from the content and the vanity that looks down on it. This vanity is expected to exert itself, to give up this freedom and to immerse it in the content, instead of merely being the arbitrary moving principle of the content: the content should be made to move itself by virtue of its own nature, i.e., through the self as its own self, and then to contemplate this movement. One should not intrude into the immanent rhythm of the Concepts[6] either arbitrarily or with wisdom gained elsewhere: such restraint is itself an essential moment of attention to the Concept.

IV. *Conclusion*

1. The exertion of the Concept

¹ "The exertion of the Concept" (*die Anstrengung des Begriffs*) is one of the odd but memorable phrases coined by Hegel. In German, too, it would be more idiomatic to speak of the exertion of conceptual thinking or conceptual analysis. But what Hegel means should be clear by now and has been commented on in several notes above.

² The close association of "pure self-movements" and "souls" may seem strange to modern readers if they are not familiar with Greek philosophy. But in Plato's *Laws*, Book X, soul is defined as the motion which can move itself (895 f.). For Hegel the Concept is even "higher" than the soul.

³ Analysis of Concepts is unwelcome both to those who are used to relying on mere notions (*Vorstellungen*)—readers who are glued, as it were, to visual aids and the comfortable vagueness of less rigorous ways of thinking—and to addicts of formalistic thinking. Hegel speaks of the latter as *dem formalen Denken, das in unwirklichen Gedanken hin und her räsonniert*. It is a kind of thinking that relies on abstractions ("unactual thoughts") which are never analyzed. Instead of devoting itself to an effort to comprehend Concepts, it juggles around abstractions.

⁴ Those who rely on notions are not aware of having a point of view: thinkers of this type forget to analyze the self and its position.

⁵ "argumentative thinking": *das Räsonnieren*.

⁶ This is the first time in the preface that we encounter Concepts (*Begriffe*) in the plural; and the plural occurs only twice after this. This is connected with the fact that Hegel associates the Concept not merely with particular concepts, though he does that, too, but also with a mode of thinking. In his usage the Concept stands for scientific philosophy, even as intuition stands for another approach which we might call romantic, notions for yet another which we might call popular, and argumentative thinking, which Hegel is about to discuss here, for a fourth type.

16. Argumentative thinking in its negative attitude—[7]

One should note the two ways in which the argumentative manner is opposed to the thinking that comprehends.[8]—First such reasoning adopts a negative attitude against its content and knows how to refute and destroy it.[9] That things are otherwise—this insight is merely negative; it is a finality that does not proceed beyond to a new content. Rather, to gain a content again one has to find something somewhere else.[10] This is the reflection into the empty ego, the vanity of its knowledge.

This vanity, however, does not only express that this content is vain but also that this insight itself is vain; for this insight is the negative that does not see what is positive in itself. By never making its own negativity its content, such reflection is never in the matter but always beyond it; therefore it imagines that with its claim of emptiness it is always more advanced than a contentful insight. On the other hand, as shown above, in the thinking that comprehends the negative belongs to the content itself and is the positive both as the immanent movement and determination of the content and as the whole of this. Seen as a result, it is the determinate negative that comes out of this movement, and thus just as much a positive content.

But considering that such thinking has a content, whether it be of notions or of thoughts or of a mixture of both, it has another side that makes comprehension difficult for it. The strange nature of this second side is closely connected with the above-mentioned essence of the idea[11]—or rather expresses it as it appears as the movement which is thinking apprehension.[12]

17. —in its positive attitude; its subject

In its negative behavior, just discussed, argumentative thinking is itself the self into which the content returns; in its positive knowledge, on the other hand, the self is a represented subject[13] to which the content is related as an accident and predicate. This subject constitutes the basis to which the content is tied and on which the movement runs back and forth.

⁷ In the original table of contents from which this heading is taken, the page reference is LXXII, but the heading clearly belongs where we have placed it, i.e., at the very top of page LXXIII. This subtitle is continued in the next one, number 17: the connection is the same as between numbers 5 and 6, and again between 9 and 10 above.

⁸ *das begreifende Denken:* see note ⁶ above; also I.1, note ³. This is the type of thinking Hegel commends.

⁹ According to Glockner (II, 464), "This is an allusion to Kant's doctrine of the unknowability of the thing in itself. Fichte already had recognized its untenability." This interpretation of Hegel's text is very questionable: the long attack on argumentative thinking is not aimed particularly at Kant, and one cannot discredit such thinking by suddenly associating it with, or blaming it for, Kant's doctrine of the unknowable thing in itself. Rather, Hegel characterizes a type of thought that argues against a rival position, "adopts a negative attitude" against that which it discusses "and knows how to refute and destroy it."

¹⁰ Glockner comments (*ibid.*): "Besides Fichte one may here think also of Jacobi insofar as he replaced the content that was not accessible to reason with faith." Again, Hegel's point seems much more general: "argumentative thinking" completely rejects the position it attacks and then has to find a new content elsewhere.

The thinking that comprehends, as Hegel suggests in the next paragraph, is constructive in its criticism. This whole discussion should be compared with I.1, paragraphs 4 and 5, and *ibid.*, note ⁹.

¹¹ *Idee.*

¹² "thinking apprehension": *denkendes Auffassen.*

¹³ *ein vorgestelltes Subjekt.*

It is different with the thinking that comprehends. The Con
cept is the object's own self which presents itself as its becom
ing; thus it is not a subject at rest[14] that carries its attribute
unmoved, but it is the Concept that moves itself and takes it
determinations back into itself. In this movement the resting
subject itself perishes:[15] it enters into the differences and the
content and constitutes the determinateness, i.e., the differen
tiated content and its movement, instead of abiding outside it
The firm ground that argumentative reasoning found in the
resting subject thus quakes, and only this movement itself be
comes the object. The subject that fills its content ceases to go
beyond that and cannot have any other predicates or attri
butes. The dispersion of the content, conversely, is bound un
der the self, and the content[16] is not something general that
free from the subject, could be assigned to several others.[1]
The content is thus in fact no longer the predicate of the sub
ject; rather it is the substance and the essence and Concept o.
that which is discussed.[18] It is of the nature of representa
tional thinking[19] to follow the attributes or predicates and to
go beyond them, quite rightly, too, because they are mere
predicates and attributes; but because that which in a propo
sition has the form of a predicate is really the substance
itself,[20] representational thinking is stopped in its advance
To represent it that way: it suffers a counterthrust.[21] Be
ginning with the subject, as if this remained the basis, it finds
because the predicate is really the substance,[20] that the sub
ject has moved into the predicate and has thus been subli
mated. Thus that which seemed to be predicate has become

[14] *Indem der Begriff das eigene Selbst des Gegenstandes ist, das sich als sein Werden darstellt, ist es nicht ein ruhendes Subjekt* . . . : "its becoming" (*sein Werden*) can refer to the self or to the object; but the following "it" (*es*) can refer only to the self.

The best commentary on all of this and a great deal of what follows is given by Hegel himself a few paragraphs later when he gives the example of the proposition: "God is being."

[15] For an illustration see the text for note [30] below.

[16] Reading: *er ist nicht* . . . , i.e., the content is not . . . (Lasson's emendation, 1907, taken over by Hoffmeister in his editions). The original edition of 1807 read: *es ist nicht* . . . , which would seem to mean that the self is not . . . In the *Werke*, in 1832 and 1841, in the only two posthumous editions before 1907, the original wording was kept.

[17] In the proposition, "God is being," which Hegel himself soon adduces as an example, being is not "something general that, free from the subject [i.e., God], could be assigned to several others."

[18] To stick to this example: being is no longer a mere predicate of the subject but said to be the substance, essence, and Concept of God.

[19] "representational thinking": *das vorstellende Denken;* a type of thinking that sticks to notions (*Vorstellungen*) instead of dealing with Concepts (*Begriffe*) like the thinking that comprehends (*das begreifende Denken*).

Heidegger contrasts representational thinking with the thinking that recalls (*das andenkende Denken*) and, unlike Hegel, seeks to move philosophy closer to poetry rather than science. (See "The Way Back into the Ground of Metaphysics," the introduction Heidegger added in 1949 to *What is Metaphysics?* in Kaufmann, *Existentialism from Dostoevsky to Sartre,* especially pp. 206 and 219.)

[20] For example, being in the proposition "God is being."

[21] *Gegenstoss:* Glockner (II, 465 f.) refers to "the important doctrine of the *counterthrust.*" He does not explain this doctrine; he merely quotes. But it seems misleading to speak of a *wichtige Lehre vom Gegenstoss.* These very abstract paragraphs may give the impression that Hegel is expounding a new and difficult doctrine, but as soon as he discusses examples a little later on, it appears that he is merely elaborating a point made earlier, in II.1: see the text following note [21], as well as notes [23] and [25] in the same section.

the whole and independent mass, and thinking can no longer stray freely but is brought to a stop by this gravity.[22]

Usually, the subject is first made the basis as the objective, fixed self, and the necessary movement to the multiplicity of the determinations or predicates proceeds from there. Here, however, this subject is replaced by the knowing ego itself, which connects the predicates and becomes the subject that holds them. The first subject[23] enters into the determination and is their soul; thus the second subject,[24] which knows, still finds in the predicate that with which it had wished to be done so it could return into itself; and instead of being in a position to function as the active element in the movement of the predicate—arguing back and forth whether this or that predicate would be suitable—the second subject is still preoccupied with the self of the content[25] and has to stay with that instead of being by itself.[26]

What has here been said can be expressed more formally: the nature of the judgment or proposition, which involves the distinction between subject and predicate, is destroyed by the speculative proposition;[27] and the identical proposition into which the former turns contains the counterthrust against that relation.[28]—This conflict between the form of a proposition and the unity of the Concept that destroys it resembles the conflict between meter and accent in rhythm. Rhythm results from the floating center and unification of both. Thus, in the philosophical proposition, too, the identity of subject and predicate is not meant to destroy the difference between both that is expressed by the form of the proposition; rather their unity is meant to emerge as a harmony. The form of the proposition is the appearance of the determinate sense, or the accent that distinguishes its fulfillment; but that the predicate expresses the substance, and the subject itself falls into the general, that is the unity in which this accent fades away.

Examples may help to explain this. In the proposition "God is being," the predicate is "being." It has substantial meaning in which the subject dissolves.[30] Being here is not meant to be a mere predicate but rather the essence, and God apparently ceases to be the firm subject, in spite of his position in the sentence.—Thinking here does not progress in the trans-

22 The weight or gravity of "being" in the proposition "God is being" stops us, and we cannot simply go on to look for other predicates.

23 "the first subject": the subject of the proposition; in our example, God.

24 "the second subject": the student.

25 That is, with the first subject, God.

26 "by itself"—and ready to go on to other things.

27 For example, "God is being." Immediately afterwards this is called an "identical proposition" because it identifies God with being.

28 The counterthrust, as we now see, is simply that what seemed to be a subject-predicate relation turns into a relation of identity, and this comes as something of a shock.

29 Cf. II.1, notes 23 and 25.

30 Cf. text for note 15 above.

tion from the subject to the predicate: the subject gets los
and thinking feels inhibited[31] and, missing the subject,
thrown back[32] to the thought of the subject. Or, because th
predicate is expressed as itself a subject, as being, as the e
sence which exhausts the nature of the subject, thinking find
the subject immediately in the predicate; and now, instead o
attaining in the predicate the free position to argue, it is sti
absorbed in the content—or at least the demand is presen
that it ought to be so absorbed.[33]

It is similar when one says: the actual is the general.[34] Th
actual as a subject vanishes in the predicate. The general i
not meant to have merely the meaning of the predicate, as i
the proposition were merely meant to say that the actual i
general. Rather, the general is supposed to express the essenc
of the actual.—Thus thinking loses the firm objective groun
it had in the subject whenever the predicate throws it back
to the subject, so that in the predicate it returns not to itse
but to the subject of the content.

This unaccustomed inhibition[36] is the main source of th
complaints about the unintelligibility of philosophical writin
—at least from those who do not lack other educational pr
requisites for understanding them. In what has here been sai
we find the reason for the specific reproach, which is ofte
heard, that many passages have to be read several times b
fore one can understand them. This is considered imprope
and it is supposed that this reproach, if well founded, is fin
and unanswerable.—From the above it should be clear wh
this amounts to. The philosophical proposition, being a prop
sition, gives rise to the opinion that the relation of subject an
predicate and the procedure of knowledge are as usual. Bu
the philosophical content destroys this procedure and th
opinion; one learns that what one supposed was not what on
was supposed to suppose;[37] and this correction of one's opin
ion requires knowledge to return to the sentence and to rein
terpret it.

One difficulty should be avoided: mixing up the speculativ
style with the argumentative style so that what is said of th
subject sometimes has the meaning of its Concept, at othe
times only the meaning of its predicate or attribute.—One styl

[31] "inhibited": *gehemmt*.

[32] "thrown back": this is the counterthrust.

[33] Instead of being free to argue about this predicate and that, one is perplexed about the meaning of Concepts.

[34] The second example is not developed at length like the first, but it shows that the point of the first example does not depend in any way on its reference to God. To be sure, other propositions about God could be added as further examples: God is love, God is spirit, God is the ground of being. But "the actual is the general" does just as well, as Hegel tries to indicate briefly.

[35] This is, once again, the counterthrust.

[36] "inhibition": *Hemmen*. See text for note [31] above.

[37] *die Meinung erfährt, dass es anders gemeint ist, als sie meinte.* Baillie quite misses Hegel's touch of humor when he translates this: "The common view discovers that the statement is intended in another sense than it is thinking of . . ."

Now that Hegel has given examples, his meaning seems clear enough to require very little commentary.

interferes with the other, and only a philosophical exposition that strictly precluded the usual relation of the parts of a sentence would attain the goal of being really vivid.

Yet non-speculative thinking also has its valid rights that are ignored in the style of the speculative proposition. That the form of the proposition is sublimated should not merely happen immediately, through the mere content of the proposition.[88] Rather, this opposite movement must be expressed; it must not be a mere internal inhibition,[39] but the return of the Concept into itself must be represented expressly. This movement which takes the place of that which proof was once supposed to accomplish is the dialectical movement of the proposition itself.[40] This alone is the actually speculative, and only the expression of this is speculative exposition. As a proposition the speculative is merely internal inhibition[39] and the failure of the essence to return into itself. Therefore we often find that philosophical expositions refer us to this internal intuition[41] and thus spare themselves the presentation of the dialectical movement of the proposition, which we demanded.

The proposition should express what the true is, but essentially this is subject; as such it is merely the dialectical movement, this way that generates itself, leads itself on, and returns into itself.[42]—In non-speculative knowledge proof constitutes this side of expressed inwardness. But since dialectic has been separated from proof, the Concept of philosophical proof has been lost.[43]

Here it may be recalled that the dialectical movement also has propositions for its parts or elements; the difficulty shown here therefore appears to recur always and to be a feature of the matter itself.[44]—This is similar to the situation in ordinary proof where the reasons used require reasons in turn, and so forth ad infinitum. Yet this form of finding reasons and conditions is a feature of those proofs which differ from dialectical movement; it belongs to external knowledge. But the element of the dialectical movement is the pure Concept;[45] thus it has a content that is through and through subject in itself. Thus no content occurs that functions as an underlying subject and receives its meaning as a predicate; the proposition is immediately a merely empty form.[46]

[38] The goal mentioned at the end of the preceding paragraph cannot be attained after all by banishing from one's prose all but speculative propositions, such as "God is being," or "the actual is the general." In these two cases, and in others like them, the content of the proposition suggests that what looks like a subject-predicate relation is really meant to be a relation of identity.

[39] See text for note [31] above.

[40] The reader must not be left to gather from the content that what looks like a predicate is not supposed to be a predicate; but this appearance of the proposition must be cancelled expressly. And this denial of what seems to have been said, this contradiction of one proposition by the next, this qualification of an assertion by what follows it, is what Hegel now introduces as "the dialectical movement."

[41] "internal intuition": the insight that attends the internal inhibition which has been mentioned a number of times.

[42] The true, being subject, is not given all at once or immediately in the form of a proposition. It develops (see II.1, note [8] above) and has to be developed in a series of propositions. In other words, as Hegel has told us before, the form of the true cannot be a single proposition but only a whole system.

[43] The dialectical progression described in note [40] above must replace proofs in philosophy. It is plainly not the same thing, and Hegel thus does not claim that in his *Phenomenology* and *Logic*, or in the philosophy of nature and the philosophy of spirit, he will prove his claims in any ordinary sense. He promises, in effect, to be rigorous, but in a somewhat novel way. Not entirely novel: soon Hegel will mention some ancient precedents.

[44] When propositions are employed to qualify propositions that went before, the same problem would seem to be inevitable at every turn.

[45] Once again, the Concept stands for a whole way of thinking. See note [6] above.

[46] See II.1, note [25] above.

Apart from the self that is intuited or represented by the senses, it is above all the name as name that designates the pure subject, the empty unit void of Concept. For this reason it may be expedient, e.g., to avoid the name "God" because this word is not immediately also a Concept but rather the proper name, the fixed repose of the underlying subject, while, e.g., being or the One, the particular, the subject, etc., also immediately suggest Concepts.[47]

Although speculative truths are formulated about this subject,[48] their content lacks the immanent Concept because it is present only as a subject at rest, and owing to this such truths easily acquire the form of mere edification.[49]—The habit of construing the speculative predicate on the model of a proposition and not as Concept and essence constitutes an obstacle that can be increased or diminished by the manner of the philosophic exposition.[50] In keeping with our insight into the nature of the speculative, the presentation should retain the dialectical form and include nothing except insofar as it is Concept and comprehended.

[47] A proper name as the subject of a proposition creates the same presumption that would be created by a noun that designates an object of sense perception; namely, that we are confronted with a fixed "underlying subject" to which some predicate is attached. Therefore, propositions about God are misleading insofar as people construe "God" as a proper name. When the subject of a proposition is being, the One, the actual, identity, quantity, becoming, the idea, or anything at all that immediately suggests a Concept, this misunderstanding is likely to be avoided.

[48] "this subject": God.

[49] For example, "God is love" and "God is spirit" are edifying propositions rather than speculative propositions. To take twentieth-century examples, Tillich's "God is being-itself" and "God is the ground of being" are at least ambiguous in this respect, and their wide appeal certainly depends on their being interpreted as edifying and inspirational.

[50] A writer can go out of his way to cultivate the audience that construes his propositions as edifying; or he can take pains to point out that he does not wish to be read that way, and that what he means is different.

[IV.2]

There is another obstacle that is as serious as the argumentative manner. The study of philosophy is obstructed no less by a conceit that does not deign to argue: one supposes that one is in possession of established truths which do not require discussion but can be assumed as the basis of what follows; one feels free to pronounce them and to judge and condemn by appealing to them. At this point it is particularly necessary that philosophy should again be made a serious pursuit. Of all sciences, arts, skills, and crafts one is convinced that mastery requires a multiple effort of learning and exercise.[1] But when it comes to philosophy, quite another prejudice is prevalent today: although one grants that having eyes and fingers is not enough to enable everyone who is given leather and tools to make shoes, it is held that everybody can immediately philosophize and judge philosophy merely because he possesses the measure in his natural reason—as if one did not equally possess the measure for a shoe in one's foot.

It seems that the mastery of philosophy is found precisely in the lack of knowledge and study, as if philosophy ceased where these begin. Philosophy is often considered a merely formal knowledge, void of content, and the insight is sadly lacking that whatever content of knowledge or science is truth does not deserve this name unless it has been produced by philosophy. Let the other sciences try to get somewhere by arguing without philosophy as much as they please: without it, they cannot contain life, spirit, or truth.

18. Natural philosophizing as healthy common sense and as genius

When it comes to real philosophy, the long path of education and the movement, as rich as it is profound, through which the spirit reaches knowledge are now considered dispensable, and the immediate revelation of the divine and a healthy common sense that has never troubled or educated itself with other knowledge or with philosophy proper are held

IV.2. There is no royal road to science

[1] Twenty years later, in the second edition of his *Encyclopedia* (1827, § 5; unchanged in the 3d edition, 1830, § 5) Hegel says very similarly: "This science [philosophy] is often treated with such contempt that even people who have taken no trouble with it express the conceit that they understand all by themselves [*von Haus aus;* literally, from home] what philosophy is all about and are able, simply on the basis of an ordinary education and especially of religious feelings, to philosophize and judge philosophy. One concedes that one has to study other sciences before one knows them, and that one is entitled to judge them only on the basis of such knowledge. One concedes that, to make a shoe, one must have learned this and it requires practice, although everybody possesses the measure for it in his foot and also his hands and in them the natural skill for the required task. Only for philosophy itself such study, learning, and trouble is not supposed to be necessary.—In recent times this comfortable opinion has received confirmation through the doctrine of immediate knowledge, knowledge by intuition."

to be just as good and as perfect a substitute as some claim chicory is for coffee.[2] It is not pleasant to remark that ignorance, indeed even crudeness that lacks form as much as taste and is incapable of concentrating thought on an abstract sentence, not to speak of the connection of several, assures us now that it is the freedom and tolerance of thought, now that it is nothing less than genius. As is well known, such genius, now the rage in philosophy, once raged no less in poetry; but when the products of such genius had any meaning at all, they were not poetry but trivial prose or, when they were more, mad oratory. Thus a supposedly natural philosophizing that considers itself too good for Concepts and thinks that this lack makes it an intuitive or visionary and poetical thinking, in fact brings to market arbitrary combinations of an imagination that has merely been disorganized by thought—fabrications that are neither flesh nor fish, neither poetry nor philosophy.[3]

Flowing along in the calmer bed of healthy common sense, natural philosophizing entertains us with a rhetoric of trivial truths. Reproached with the insignificance of all this, it assures us that meaning and fulfillment reside in its heart and must reside in other hearts, too—and one supposes that such references to the innocence of the heart, the purity of conscience, *et al.*, represent final matters which brook no objections or further demands. But the task was not to leave the best deep inside but to bring it to light out of these depths. To produce final truths of that sort was trouble one might easily have spared oneself, for it has long been easy to find them in the catechism, in popular proverbs, etc.[4]

It is not difficult to show how indeterminate and vague, or how misleading, such truths are, or even to show to consciousness how it also contains diametrically opposite truths.[5] As consciousness tries to extricate itself from this confusion it is likely to fall into new confusions[6] and may finally expostulate that as a matter of fact things are thus and thus while those supposed truths are sophistries. "Sophistries" is a slogan that common sense likes to use against educated reason, even as ignorance of philosophy likes to apply the expression "idle dreams" to philosophy.

Those who invoke feeling as their internal oracle are fin-

² For once, one of Hegel's long sentences has not been broken up in translation; but many of his sentences are a great deal longer than this one. Hegel, incidentally, loved coffee and despised substitutes (cf., e.g., his letter of April 29, 1814, in D).

³ Here the great difference between Hegel and Heidegger, referred to above (IV.1, note ¹⁹), becomes quite explicit.

Toward the end of the preface, Hegel made some use of notes which Rosenkranz called "Aphorisms from the Jena Period" when he published them in 1844 near the end of his Hegel biography. The numbers I use for reference were assigned by Hoffmeister when he reprinted these notes under the same title in 1936 in *Dokumente zu Hegels Entwicklung*. The main examples will be cited below. At this point one of the aphorisms seems relevant although one cannot truly say that Hegel "used" it:

"The truth of science is a calm light that illuminates and delights everything, like the warmth in which everything simultaneously flourishes and explicates the internal treasures in the breadth of life. A *flash of inspiration* [*Gedankenblitz*: a common German word, comparable to "brain storm" and stylistically suggestive of aphorisms] is the Capaneus who . . . cannot attain enduring life" (#23).

Capaneus, one of the Seven against Thebes, defied Zeus who struck him dead with a lightning bolt.

⁴ The task of philosophy is not to compete with popular proverbs or religious wisdom but to supplant notions with Concepts, intuition with science.

⁵ Appeals to common sense can often be met by appealing to common sense on behalf of "diametrically opposite truths."

⁶ "new confusions": Hegel says "new ones" which could also mean "new truths," in which case, of course, "truths" would be meant ironically. In context the sense of the passage remains unaffected by this ambiguity.

ished with anyone who does not agree: they have to own that
they have nothing further to say to anyone who does not find
and feel the same in his heart—in other words, they trample
under foot the roots of humanity. For it is the nature of humanity to struggle for agreement with others, and humanity
exists only in the accomplished community of consciousness.
The anti-human, the animalic consists in remaining at the level
of feeling and being able to communicate only through feelings.[7]

If someone asked for a royal road to science, no road could
be more comfortable than this: to rely on healthy common
sense and, in order to progress with the times and with philosophy, to read reviews of philosophic essays, at most the
prefaces and first paragraphs; for the latter offer the general
principles, which are all-important, and the former, in addition
to a historical notice, also some judgment which, being a judgment, goes beyond what is judged.[8] This vulgar road can be
taken in one's dressing gown; but the elevated feeling of the
eternal, the holy, and the infinite struts about in a high priest's
robes—on a road that[9] itself is immediate being at the core,
the genius of profound and original ideas and lofty flashes of
inspiration.[10] Yet even as such profundity still does not reveal
the fount of essence, so, too, such rockets are not yet the
empyrean.[11] True thoughts and scientific insight are to be
won only through the work of the Concept. This alone can
produce the generality of knowledge which is neither the common vagueness and paltriness of common sense, but educated
and complete knowledge, nor the uncommon generality of the
disposition of reason that has corrupted itself through laziness
and the conceit of genius, but truth that has developed into its
native form—and is thus capable of being owned by all self-
conscious reason.

⁷ Once again Hegel returns to a theme introduced early in the preface. Cf. I.3, especially note ¹⁵. But this paragraph near the end is singularly eloquent in its insistence that irrationalism, whether religious or romantic, destroys "the roots of humanity." In the twentieth century it has become fashionable to associate Kierkegaard and existentialism with humanity and to consider Hegel the archetype of the inhuman thinker. Hegel himself sees reason and exoteric scientific procedures as the ground of humanity and points out that those who spurn reason are driven also to spurn communication with those who do not feel what they feel.

⁸ In his commentary on Euclid (Book II, Chapter 4), Proclus reports how Pharaoh Ptolemy I wanted to study geometry without going through the thirteen parts of Euclid's book; he wanted a short cut. But Euclid replied: "There is no royal road to geometry."

This passage makes use of two of Hegel's posthumously published "Aphorisms": "The usual royal road in philosophy is to read the prefaces and reviews in order to get an approximate notion of the matter" (#52). "The last royal road for the student is to think for himself" (#53).

⁹ Here one might interpolate: does not lead to but . . .

¹⁰ *Gedankenblitze:* see note ³ above.

¹¹ Here Hegel uses "Aphorism" #9: "Even as there was a language of genius in poetry, the present seems to be the *philosophical period of geniuses*. A little carbon, oxygen, nitrogen, and hydrogen kneaded together [*zusammengeknetet*] and stuck into a piece of paper on which others have written about polarity, etc., rockets shot into the air with a wooden pigtail of vanity, they suppose that they represent the empyrean. Thus Görres, Wagner, *et al.* The crudest empirism [*Empirie*] with the formalism of materials and poles, embellished with analogies devoid of reason and boozy [*besoffenen*] flashes of inspiration."

19. Conclusion: the author's relation to the public

[IV.3]

I find the distinctive mark of science in the self-movement
of the Concept but have to admit that the above-mentioned,
as well as several other peripheral, features of the notions of
our time about the nature and form of truth are different and
indeed quite opposed to my view. It would therefore seem
that an attempt to present the System of Science from this
point of view is not likely to meet with a favorable reception.
But[1] there are other considerations. Occasionally, e.g., the
excellence of Plato's philosophy was supposed to be due to
his scientifically worthless myths; but there have also been
times, which are even called times of wild enthusiasm, when
Aristotle's philosophy was esteemed for its speculative profundity and Plato's *Parmenides,* probably the greatest work
of art of ancient dialectic, was considered the true disclosure
and the positive expression of the divine life, and in spite of
the frequent turbidity of the products of ecstasy, this misunderstood ecstasy was in fact supposed to be nothing less than
the pure Concept. Furthermore, what has excellence in the
philosophy of our time finds its own value in being scientific
and although others understand this differently, it is only
through this scientific posture that it actually gains credit.
Therefore I can also hope that this attempt to vindicate science
for the Concept and to present it in this, its proper, element
may win acceptance through the inner truth of the matter.
We must have the conviction that it is of the nature of truth
to prevail when its time has come, and that truth appears only
when its time has come—and therefore never appears too
early, nor ever finds that the public is not ready for it.[2] And
the individual needs public acceptance to prove the truth of
what is as yet his solitary concern; he needs to see how the
conviction that is as yet particular becomes general. But at
this point the public must often be distinguished from those
who act as if they were its representatives and spokesmen. In

IV.3. The philosopher and the public

[1] The passage from the first [1] to the second [1] forms a single sentence in the original. Hegel's tribute to Plato's *Parmenides,* which is amplified in Hegel's lectures on the history of philosophy, is in the Neoplatonic tradition and indebted to Proclus.

[2] This is reminiscent of an earlier passage in the preface: see the text for III.3, note [6]. But the present formulation is more extreme, and its strikingly untragic conclusion is plainly untenable. Hegel's later conception of world-historical individuals, of which note [28] in III.3 above gives at least some idea, is not quite so objectionable. Hegel's supreme confidence in the passage to which the present note refers is obviously based on his own case: he has no doubt that the time has come for his type of philosophy. And although he was then, at the age of thirty-six, still very little known, and though the first review of the *Phenomenology* did not appear until almost two full years after the publication of the book, Hegel's confidence was astonishingly justified within much less than two decades—to repeat, in his own case.

some respects the public behaves differently from these people, even in the opposite way. When a philosophical essay is not found appealing, the public may good-naturedly ascribe the fault to itself, but the others,[3] sure of their competence, ascribe the sole fault to the author. In the public the effect is quieter than the activity of these dead men when they bury their dead.[4]

The general level of insight now is more educated, curiosity is wide awake, and judgments are made more quickly than formerly; so the feet of them which shall carry thee out are already at the door.[5] But from this we must often distinguish the slower effect which corrects the attention that was extorted by imposing assurances as well as disdainful reproaches: some writers find an audience only after a time, while others after a time have none any more.[6]

In our time general participation in the life of the spirit has been greatly strengthened, and every particular, as is fitting, counts for that much less. Moreover, this vast public clings to and demands its full extent and the wealth of its education; so the share of the total work of the spirit that can be assigned to the activity of any individual has to be small. Hence the individual—and this is in any case in keeping with the nature of science—should forget himself that much more. To be sure, he should become and do what he can; but less should be demanded of him, even as he must expect less of himself and demand less for himself.[7]

3 Those who pose as spokesmen.

4 "Follow me; and let the dead bury their dead" (Matthew 8:22). The would-be spokesmen are spiritually as dead as most of the books they review and bury.

5 "The feet of them which have buried thy husband are at the door, and shall carry thee out" (Acts 5:9). Hegel assumes as he is writing in his study that there is no dearth of people outside who are ready to bury his book as soon as it is published.

6 In the original this whole paragraph forms a single sentence which ends: ". . . *und einem Teile eine Mitwelt erst in einiger Zeit gibt, während ein anderer nach dieser keine Nachwelt mehr hat.*" *Mitwelt*, literally "with-world," and *Nachwelt*, literally "after-world," are common nouns that mean, respectively, one's contemporaries and coming generations. More literally, then, Hegel says that some are given a with-world only after a time (the tragic possiblities implicit in this admission are not noted expressly), while others, after a time, have no after-world any more.

7 The final paragraph also forms a single sentence in the original. It spells out another implication of Hegel's insistence that philosophy should attain the level of a science. While he is confident that the time has come for what he has to offer and that his philosophy will, after a while, gain wide acceptance, he does not infer from this that he himself is important. A philosopher should forget his own person, devote himself to his subject matter, "and do what he can."

"Who Thinks Abstractly?"

In the nineteenth-century edition of Hegel's *Werke,* this article (*Wer denkt abstrakt?*) appears in volume XVII, 400–5. Rosenkranz discusses it briefly (355 f.) and says that it shows "how much Hegel . . . entered into the Berlin manner."

Glockner reprints it in his edition of the *Werke* in vol. XX (1930), which is entitled: *Vermischte Schriften aus der Berliner Zeit.*[1] He includes it among "four *feuilletons* that Hegel wrote for local papers during the later years of his Berlin period." But Glockner admits: "The exact place of publication is unfortunately unknown to me" (xix).

Hoffmeister, whose critical edition of Hegel's *Berliner Schriften: 1818–1831* (1956) is much more comprehensive than Glockner's (800 pages versus 550), does not include this article. In a footnote he says that it belongs to Hegel's "Jena period (1807/08)" (xiii). This is an uncharacteristic slip: at the beginning of 1807 Hegel went to Bamberg, in 1808 to Nürnberg; and in the first weeks of 1807, before he left Jena, he certainly lacked the time and peace of mind to write this article.

Of Glockner's "four *feuilletons*" Hoffmeister retains only one, and that is really a letter to a newspaper, protesting their review of a new play. Hoffmeister gives no reasons for dating this article so much earlier than Rosenkranz and Glockner did. Possibly, the disparaging remark about Kotzebue (a German playwright, 1761–1819) suggests a date before Kotzebue was stabbed to death by a German theology student. That the piece was written in Jena seems most unlikely: it is so very different from the articles—and the *Phenomenology*—that Hegel wrote

[1] "Diverse Writings of the Berlin Period."

during his harassed and unhappy years in that city. But Hoffmeister could be right that it was written in 1807 or 1808.

WHO THINKS ABSTRACTLY?

Think? Abstractly?—*Sauve qui peut!* Let those who can save
themselves! Even now I can hear a traitor, bought by the
enemy, exclaim these words, denouncing this essay because it
will plainly deal with metaphysics. For *metaphysics* is a word,
no less than *abstract,* and almost *thinking* as well, from which
everybody more or less runs away as from a man who has
caught the plague.

But the intention here really is not so wicked, as if the
meaning of thinking and of abstract were to be explained
here. There is nothing the beautiful world finds as intolerable
as explanations. I, too, find it terrible when somebody begins
to explain, for when worst comes to worst I understand everything myself. Here the explanation of thinking and abstract
would in any case be entirely superfluous; for it is only because
the beautiful world knows what it means to be abstract that
it runs away. Just as one does not desire what one does not
know, one also cannot hate it. Nor is it my intent to try craftily
to reconcile the beautiful world with thinking or with the
abstract as if, under the semblance of small talk, thinking and
the abstract were to be put over till in the end they had found
their way into society incognito, without having aroused any
disgust; even as if they were to be adopted imperceptibly by
society, or, as the Swabians say, *hereingezäunselt,* before the
author of this complication suddenly exposed this strange
guest, namely the abstract, whom the whole party had long
treated and recognized under a different title as if he were a
good old acquaintance. Such scenes of recognition which are
meant to instruct the world against its will have the inexcusable
fault that they simultaneously humiliate, and the wirepuller
tries with his artifice to gain a little fame; but this humiliation

and this vanity destroy the effect, for they push away again an instruction gained at such a price.

In any case, such a plan would be ruined from the start, for it would require that the crucial word of the riddle is not spoken at the outset. But this has already happened in the title. If this essay toyed with such craftiness, these words should not have been allowed to enter right in the beginning; but like the cabinet member in a comedy, they should have been required to walk around during the entire play in their overcoat, unbuttoning it only in the last scene, disclosing the flashing star of wisdom. The unbuttoning of the metaphysical overcoat would be less effective, to be sure, than the unbuttoning of the minister's: it would bring to light no more than a couple of words, and the best part of the joke ought to be that it is shown that society has long been in possession of the matter itself; so what they would gain in the end would be the mere name, while the minister's star signifies something real—a bag of money.

That everybody present should know what thinking is and what is abstract is presupposed in good society, and we certainly are in good society. The question is merely *who* thinks abstractly. The intent, as already mentioned, is not to reconcile society with these things, to expect it to deal with something difficult, to appeal to its conscience not frivolously to neglect such a matter that befits the rank and status of beings gifted with reason. Rather it is my intent to reconcile the beautiful world with itself, although it does not seem to have a bad conscience about this neglect; still, at least deep down, it has a certain respect for abstract thinking as something exalted, and it looks the other way not because it seems too lowly but because it appears too exalted, not because it seems too mean but rather too noble, or conversely because it seems an *Espèce*, something special; it seems something that does not lend one distinction in general society, like new clothes, but rather something that—like wretched clothes, or rich ones if they are decorated with precious stones in ancient mounts or embroidery that, be it ever so rich, has long become quasi-Chinese—excludes one from society or makes one ridiculous in it.

Who thinks abstractly? The uneducated, not the educated. Good society does not think abstractly because it is too easy, because it is too lowly (not referring to the external status)— not from an empty affectation of nobility that would place itself above that of which it is not capable, but on account of the inward inferiority of the matter.

The prejudice and respect for abstract thinking are so great that sensitive nostrils will begin to smell some satire or irony at this point; but since they read the morning paper they know that there is a prize to be had for satires and that I should therefore sooner earn it by competing for it than give up here without further ado.

I have only to adduce examples for my proposition: everybody will grant that they confirm it. A murderer is led to the place of execution. For the common populace he is nothing but a murderer. Ladies perhaps remark that he is a strong, handsome, interesting man. The populace finds this remark terrible: What? A murderer handsome? How can one think so wickedly and call a murderer handsome; no doubt, you yourselves are something not much better! This is the corruption of morals that is prevalent in the upper classes, a priest may add, knowing the bottom of things and human hearts.

One who knows men traces the development of the criminal's mind: he finds in his history, in his education, a bad family relationship between his father and mother, some tremendous harshness after this human being had done some minor wrong, so he became embittered against the social order —a first reaction to this that in effect expelled him and henceforth did not make it possible for him to preserve himself except through crime.—There may be people who will say when they hear such things: he wants to excuse this murderer! After all I remember how in my youth I heard a mayor lament that writers of books were going too far and sought to extirpate Christianity and righteousness altogether; somebody had written a defense of suicide; terrible, really too terrible!— Further questions revealed that *The Sufferings of Werther* [by Goethe, 1774] were meant.

This is abstract thinking: to see nothing in the murderer

except the abstract fact that he is a murderer, and to annul all other human essence in him with this simple quality.

It is quite different in refined, sentimental circles—in Leipzig. There they strewed and bound flowers on the wheel and on the criminal who was tied to it.—But this again is the opposite abstraction. The Christians may indeed trifle with Rosicrucianism, or rather cross-rosism, and wreathe roses around the cross. The cross is the gallows and wheel that have long been hallowed. It has lost its one-sided significance of being the instrument of dishonorable punishment and, on the contrary, suggests the notion of the highest pain and the deepest rejection together with the most joyous rapture and divine honor. The wheel in Leipzig, on the other hand, wreathed with violets and poppies, is a reconciliation à la Kotzebue, a kind of slovenly sociability between sentimentality and badness.

In quite a different manner I once heard a common old woman who worked in a hospital kill the abstraction of the murderer and bring him to life for honor. The severed head had been placed on the scaffold, and the sun was shining. How beautifully, she said, the sun of God's grace shines on Binder's head!—You are not worthy of having the sun shine on you, one says to a rascal with whom one is angry. This woman saw that the murderer's head was struck by the sunshine and thus was still worthy of it. She raised it from the punishment of the scaffold into the sunny grace of God, and instead of accomplishing the reconciliation with violets and sentimental vanity, saw him accepted in grace in the higher sun.

Old woman, your eggs are rotten! the maid says to the market woman. What? she replies, my eggs rotten? You may be rotten! You say that about my eggs? You? Did not lice eat your father on the highways? Didn't your mother run away with the French, and didn't your grandmother die in a public hospital? Let her get a whole shirt instead of that flimsy scarf; we know well where she got that scarf and her hats: if it were not for those officers, many wouldn't be decked out like that these days, and if their ladyships paid more attention to their households, many would be in jail right now. Let her mend the holes in her stockings!—In brief, she does not leave one whole thread on her. She thinks abstractly and subsumes the other woman—scarf, hat, shirt, etc., as well as her fingers and other parts of her, and her father and whole family, too —solely under the crime that she has found the eggs rotten. Everything about her is colored through and through by these rotten eggs, while those officers of which the market woman spoke—if, as one may seriously doubt, there is anything to that—may have got to see very different things.

To move from the maid to a servant, no servant is worse off than one who works for a man of low class and low income; and he is better off the nobler his master is. The common man again thinks more abstractly, he gives himself noble airs vis-à-vis the servant and relates himself to the other man merely as to a servant; he clings to this one predicate. The servant is best off among the French. The nobleman is familiar with his servant, the Frenchman is his friend. When they are alone, the servant does the talking: see Diderot's *Jacques et son maître;* the master does nothing but take snuff and see what time it is and lets the servant take care of everything else. The nobleman knows that the servant is not merely a servant, but also knows the latest city news, the girls, and harbors good suggestions; he asks him about these matters, and the servant may say what he knows about these questions. With a French master, the servant may not only do this; he may also broach a subject, have his own opinions and insist on them; and when the master wants something, it is not done with an order but he has to argue and convince the servant of his opinion and add a good word to make sure that this opinion retains the upper hand.

In the army we encounter the same difference. Among the Austrians a soldier may be beaten, he is canaille; for whatever has the passive right to be beaten is canaille. Thus the common soldier is for the officer this *abstractum* of a beatable subject with whom a gentleman who has a uniform and *port d'epée* must trouble himself—and that could drive one to make a pact with the devil.

Index

This Index covers both *Hegel: A Reinterpretation* and *Hegel: Texts and Commentary*.

Arabic numerals refer to *sections* of the former, not pages. D indicates references to Chapter VII (Documentation, arranged chronologically) and is followed by the year. An asterisk indicates a letter written by, or addressed to, the person listed.

References beginning with a Roman numeral will be found in the latter volume, which is divided into 12 sections, I.1 through IV.3.

By including first names, the Index should help to identify some persons mentioned in passing in the text.

P means Preface. "Who Thinks Abstractly" (in *Texts and Commentary*) has not been indexed because it is so short; neither has the Bibliography.

Abraham, 64
absolute, 49, I.3, II.1; absolute ego, D1795; absolute idea, I.3
accidental and incidental, 62
Achenwall, Gottfried, 51
Acts, Book of, IV.3
actual, 49, 61, II.1, IV.1
actual, the spirit alone is the, II.1
Aegina, sculptures, 53
Aeschylus, 6, 21, 65
Afterdienst (Kant), 5
afterlife, D1854
Agathon, D1835
Ahndung, Ahnung, III.3
Alexander the Great, 16, 27, 60, 62
alienation, 7, 14
allusiveness, 28, 29

Altenstein, Karl Sigmund Franz, Freiherr vom Stein zum, 41, D1817*
America, 1, 13
Anaxagoras, 30, 34, III.3
Anschauung, 34, 65, D1807, I.2, III.3
Anselm, St., 66
an sich, 7, 34, II.1
Anstrengung des Begriffs, IV.1
Antigone, see Sophocles
antinomies, 19, 42, 44
antithesis, thesis & synthesis, 36, III.3. See also dialectic
an und für sich, II.1
Anytus, 4
Apelles, 14
Apollo, 6, 20

Appian, III.2
applause, III.3
Aquinas, St. Thomas, 66, 70
Arabic Philosophy, 66
Archilochus, 18
argue, not deign to, III.2
Aristophanes, D1835
Aristotle, P, 4, 16, 20, 21, 24, 25, 27, 30, 32, 34, 37, 42, 47, 59–61, 65–67, 70, D1814, I.3, III.3, IV.1, IV.3
Asverus, Ludwig Christoph Ferdinand, D1806
ataraxia, 18, 35
atheism, 26
aufheben, aufgehoben, 7, 12, 34, 42, II.1, II.3, III.1, IV.1
Augustine, St., 13
Aurelius, Marcus, 33
Ausbildung, 7
auswendig, III.2
Autenrieth, Johann Hermann Ferdinand von, D1807
Avineri, Shlomo, 58

Baader, Franz, D1816
bacchanalian whirl, III.3
Bach, Johann Sebastian, 27
Bachmann, Karl Friedrich, 27, D1810
Bacon, Francis, 66
Bähr, L., 4
Baillie, J. B., 30, 31, 33, 34, I.1, I.2, II.1, II.2, II.3, III.1, IV.1
Bamberger Zeitung, 40
Barbarossa, 62
Bartlett's *Familiar Quotations*, 2
Baumgarten, Alexander Gottlieb, 51
beauty & understanding, I.3
becoming, 46, I.1, II.1
becomes itself, II.1
Beer, Heinrich, D1854
Beethoven, Ludwig van, 1, 27
Begriff, see also Concept, 14, 34, I.1, I.3, IV.1
Begriffs, der Ernst des, I.1
being, 46, 47, II.1, III.1
bekannt, II.3
Berkeley, George, 66, I.1, II.3
better versus good, D1810, D1813
Beyer, W. R., 68
bifurcation, 14

Bildung, 36, I.3, II.3, III.3
Bildungsroman, 1, I.3; *Bildungsroman of the Weltgeist*, 34
Böhme, Jacob, 66, D1870
Bosanquet, Bernard, 68
Bradley, F. H., 68
Brentano, Clemens, 50
Brentano, Franz, 35
British Idealism, 52, 68
Brownian System, D1816
Buber, Martin, 11
bud, blossom & fruit, 31, I.1
Bultmann, Rudolf, 65
Bunsen, Christian Karl Josias Frhr. von, 70
Burkhardt, Christiana Charlotte Johanna, 23
Burkhardt, Ludwig, 23
Butler, E. M., *The Tyranny of Greece over Germany*, 21

Caesar, Julius, 60, 62, III.1; year of birth, III.2, III.3
Camus, Albert, P
Capaneus, IV.2
Carnap, Rudolf, 47
Cart, Jean Jacques, 11
Cassirer, Ernst, 2
catechism, IV.2
categories, 42–44, 46
catholicism, D1807
Ceres, 15
Charlemagne, 62
Chinese and Indian philosophy, 66
Christian, dog the best, 55
Christianity, 28, 33, 34, 59, 65, D1796
Cicero, 4, 15, 42
circle, II.3
circle, the true as a, 56, II.1
Cless, Heinrich David von, 4
coffee, D1814, IV.2
coin, truth is not a minted, III.1
Collingwood, R. G., 68, II.2
Collins, James, *The Mind of Kierkegaard*, III.1
collisions, 64
common sense, 14, 16, 17, II.3, IV.2
Communists, 64
Concept, 19, 34, 67, 68, D1807, I.1, I.2, I.3, II.3, III.2, III.3,

Concept (*cont'd*)
IV.1; Concept versus concept, 14, 19
concrete, 67
counterthrust, IV.1
Cousin, Victor, 68
criticism, internal, II.1
criticism, philosophical, I.1
Criticism, New, 68
Crito, 4
Croce, Benedetto, 68
crucifixion, II.3
cultus spurius (Kant), 5
cunning of reason, 62, III.3

Dante, 27, 28
Darius, 60
Darwin, Charles, 31
Dasein, 45, III.2; equated with *In-der-Zeit-Sein*, 67
Daub, Karl, 4, D1816*
death himself, Hegel as, 18
Declaration of Independence, 1
deduction versus comprehension, 17
Democritus, 18
Demosthenes, 4
Denken, das andenkende, IV.1
Denken, das begreifende, IV.1
depth, empty, I.2
Desan, Wilfred, 68
Descartes, René, 30, 37, 60, 66, I.1
develop, 67
Dewey, John, 68
dialectic: espec., 37, 42–46, 49, 68, IV.1
dialectic, ancient, IV.3
Diderot, Denis, *Rameau's Nephew*, 30
differentiation, III.3
Dilthey, Wilhelm, 68
Diogenes, 30
Diogenes Laertius, 18, 21, 37
Dionysian whirl, III.3
Dionysus Zagreus, II.3
disagreement, philosophical, 18, 67, I.1
dismemberment, absolute, II.3
divination, III.3
dog the best Christian, 55
dogmatism, 19, II.1, III.1, III.3. See also propositions and God
Dostoevsky, F. M., 22

dragon seed of Hegelian pantheism, 69
dreams, 14, I.2
Dryden, John, 37

Eberhard, Johann August, 51
Eckermann, Johann Peter, 33, 36
ecstasy, I.2
edification, 7, 62, D1816, I.2
education, ancient & modern, II.3
ego, absolute, D1795
ego, non-ego, D1795
ego, pure, I.3
Einstein on God, 62
Eliot, George, 66
embryo, II.1
empiricism, scientific, 19
Endel, Nanette, D1797*, D1798*
en soi, II.1
entzweit, Entzweiung, 14, III.2
Epictetus, 4
Epicureans, 66
Erasmus, Desiderius, 22
Erdmann, Johann Eduard, 68, D1880
erkannt, II.3
esoteric, 16, D1795, I.3
essence and form, II.1
eternal life, D1796
Euclid, III.2, IV.2
Euripides, 4, 6, 18, 21
Evans, Arthur, 53
Evans, Mary Ann, 66
excellent will get itself used, III.3
excuse versus justify, D1811
exegetical thinking, P
existentialism, P, 60, 64, IV.2; term coined by Schelling, 39. See also Heidegger, Jaspers, Kierkegaard, Sartre
exoteric, 16, I.3

false, III.1
familiar, II.3
feeling, I.2, IV.2
Feuerbach, Ludwig, 66, D1840*
Fichte, Johann Gottlieb, 4, 5, 7, 14, 16, 20, 21, 23–27, 35–37, 39, 41, 42, 56, 58, 66, D1795, D1804, D1817, II.1, III.1, III.3, IV.1; *Critique of All Revelation*, 5, 26, D1795; *Sun-clear Report to the Larger Public about the*

Fichte, Johann Gottlieb (cont'd)
  Real Nature of the Newest Philosophy: An Attempt to Compel the Reader to Understand, 26, I.1, III.3; System der Sittenlehre, 14, 21, 26, 56; Vocation of Man, 26; Vocation of the Scholar, D1795; Wissenschaftslehre, 17, 26, D1795; Report on the Concept of the Wissenschaftslehre and Its Fate so far, 26
Findlay, John N., Hegel, P, 37, 57, 65, Chapter VIII motto
finite, III.1
Fischer, Kuno, P, 29, 39, 53, 68, 70
Forberg, F. K., 26
for itself, 7, II.1, II.3
formalism, 39, D1805, D1807, I.3, III.3
form and essence, II.1
forms of consciousness, 34, 35, II.3, III.1
Formtrieb, 7
for us, II.1
France, 1
freedom, 3, 59, 62, 63, D1795
freedom tree, 3
French, D1807
French Revolution, 1, 3, 16, 26, 37, D1807, I.3
Freud, Sigmund, 7, 33, 46
Friedrich Wilhelm III and IV, 70
Fries, J. F., 23, 24, 41, 66, D1805
Fromm, Erich, 9
Frommann, Karl Friedrich Ernst, 23, D1807, D1816*
für sich, 7, II.1, II.3
Fuhrmans, Horst, 39, 68

Gabler, Georg Andreas, 22
Gans, Eduard, 53, D1827*
Gedankenblitz, IV.2
Gegenstoss, IV.1
Gehäuse, 28
Geist, 7, 22, 34, 65, II.1. See also spirit
Geist, der heilige, 34, III.1
general, I.1, I.3
genius, IV.2
geometry, III.2
German, teach philosophy to speak, D1805

Germany, 1
Gestalt, 7, 34
Gestalten des Bewusstseins, 34, 35, II.3, III.1
Gibbon, Edward, 2
Glockner, Hermann, Hegel, P, 4, 15, 21, 23, 24, 31, 38, 53, 66, Chapter VIII motto, III.2, III.3, IV.1
God, 5, 17, 61, 62, 65, D1795, D1799, I.2, II.3; as substance, II.1; avoiding the name of, IV.1; before the Creation, 42; death of, 20, 34; moral proof of, D1795; proofs of his existence, D1812; propositions about, II.1, IV.1
Goebhardt, Josef Anton, 22, D1806, D1807
Goethe, Johann, Wolfgang von, P, 1–3, 5–7, 14, 23, 24, 31, 33, 36, 42, 60, 65, 68, D1795, D1798*, D1799, D1803*, D1805, D1807, D1810, D1820, D1825*, D1827, D1831*, D1832*, D1835, D1870; Faust, 1, 27–29, 33, 34, 36, 65, D1812, I.1, II.3, III.3; Gespräche cited, D1827; Iphigenia, 1, 3, 6, 7, 10, 30, 65; Wilhelm Meister, 1, 26, 34, 37, I.3
Gogel, Johann Noë, D1796
Golgotha, 20, 34
Good Friday, speculative, 20, 34
Görres, Johann Joseph von, IV.2
Gothic temple, D1795
gravitation, III.2
Greeks, 3, 7, 8, 21, 65, D1794. See also individual names
Greek sculpture, 53, D1835
Greek philosophy in Hegel's History of Philosophy, 66
Green, T. H., 66, 68
Grillparzer, Franz, D1853*, D1855*
Grundsatz, 14, II.1
Gutzkow, Karl, D1870*

Haering, Theodor, Hegel, P, 38, III.1
half-truths, 14
Haller von Hallerstein, Johann, Sigmund Freiherr von, D1810
Hamilton, William, 66

Handel, G. F., 27
happiness versus contentment, D1811
harmony, 6, 7, 14, 27
Hartmann, Nicolai, 48
Hauslehrer, 5
Haydn, Franz Josef, 1, 27
Haym, Rudolf, *Hegel*, P, 21, 22, 27, 30, 40, Chapter VIII motto
head, walk on, II.2
Hegel as a lecturer, 22, 24, 52–55, D1816 (3 letters), D1827, D1835, D1840, D1870; father's death, D1799; Hegel's philosophy represents its age and requires modification as new discoveries are made, D1827
Hegel, articles in *Critical Journal of Philosophy*, 14, 16–22, 39; *Difference of the Fichtean and Schellingian System of Philosophy*, 14, 26; "Eleusis" (poem), 10, D1796; *Encyclopedia*, P, 19, 37, 38, 40, 42, 43, 45, 46, 49, 51–58, 65, 66, II.1; "Faith and Knowledge", 6, 20, 21, 34, 55; "German Constitution", 21; *History of Philosophy*, P, 66–67, I.1; *Logic*, P, 19, 22, 37, 38, 40, 42–52, 56, 58, 61, 67, D1812, D1816, II.3, III.1, III.3, IV.1; "Natural Right", 21, 38; *Phenomenology of the Spirit*, P, 1, 6, 7, 8, 10, 13, 14, 16, 18–43, 46, 48, 51, 52, 55, 56–58, 61, 64, D1806, D1807, D1809, D1814, and Chapter VIII entire; *Philosophy of History*, P, 53, 59–65, D1827; *Philosophy of Right*, P, 1, 14, 21, 29, 37, 38, 40, 42, 52, 58, 61, 63, D1827, II.1; "Positivity of the Christian Religion", 9, 12, 20, 60, 61; *Propädeutik*, 40, 51; *Realphilosophie*, 22; *System der Sittlichkeit*, 21; *Theologische Jugendschriften*, 4, 8–10, 12–13, 20, 60, 61; translation of Cart's *Confidential Letters*, 11; *Vernunft in der Geschichte*, 59–65; "Who Thinks Abstractly", 21, Chapter IX
Hegel, Christiane, 41, D1799*, D1814*, D1815*, D1831*,
D1832* (1st item in D)
Hegel, Karl, 23, 53
Hegel, Marie, 41, D1811*, D1829*, D1831*
Heidegger, Martin, P, 28, 35, 47, 60, 67, IV.1, IV.2
Heine Heinrich, 26, D1835*, D1838*, D1854*
Helvetius, C. A., 2
Henning, Leopold von, 52
Heraclitus, 27, II.3
Herbart, Johann Friedrich, 5
Herder, Johann Gottfried, 35, 56, D1795
heresy, D1795
Hermes, Johann Thimoteus, *Sophiens Reise*, 4
Herrick, M. T., 37
Hesse, Hermann, I.3
Herz, Markus, 35
Hinrichs, H. F. W., *The Essence of Ancient Tragedy*, 36; Hegel's *Vorrede*, 55; Hegel letter to, preface to Chapter VIII
history, 28, Chapter VI; and the accidental, III.2, III.3; versus duration, D1813
Hobbes, Thomas, 66, I.1
Hoffmeister, Johannes, 3, 4, 30, 35, 52, 54, 60, 66, II.1, III.3, IV.2
Holbein, Hans, 22
Hölderlin, Friedrich, P, 1, 2, 4–6, 10, 60, 65, D1794*, D1795*, D1796*, D1803, D1804, D1807
Homburg, Count of, D1804
Homer, 4, 14, 30, 60, D1805
Hook, Sidney, *From Hegel to Marx*, 58
Horace cited, 46
horos, I.2
Hotho, Heinrich Gustav, 53, D1835*
Hübscher, Arthur, 4
Humanität, 6
humanity, IV.2
Hume, David, 19, 65, 66, I.1
Husserl, Edmund, 35, 60
Hyppolite, Jean, 13, 29

idea, D1807
idea as species, III.3
idealism, II.1, III.3
immediacy, 42, 44, II.1, II.3

in and for itself, II.1
inclinations, 2
Indian and Chinese philosophy, 66
infinite, III.1; infinity, two types, 7
in itself, II.1
insight, III.2
intelligibility, I.3
intensity void of content, I.2
intimation, III.3
intuition, 34, I.2, III.3, D1807
inwendig, III.2
Iphigenia, see Goethe
Isaiah, 28
Islam, 65
Isocrates, 4

Jacob's dream, II.2
Jacobi, F. H., 18–20, 41, 66, D1795, D1812, D1816, I.2, IV.1
James, William, 29, 68
Jaspers, D1812; *Psychologie der Weltanschauungen*, 28, 31
Jesus, 8–10, 13, 33, 40, 64
Job, Book of, 3, 60
Johnson, Dr., II.3
Joshua, 26
Judaism, 65

Kant, Immanuel, 1–3, 5–10, 14, 16–21, 23–28, 30–32, 34, 35, 37, 39, 41, 42, 44, 46, 48, 51, 52, 54–58, 62, 64, 66, 70, D1794, D1795, D1812, I.1, II.1, III.3, III.3, IV.1; *Anthropology*, 2, 7; *Critique of Practical Reason*, 7, 17, 35, 36; *Critique of Pure Reason*, 3, 5, 7, 26, 51, 56, D1812, III.3; *Grundlegung*, 7, 21; *Idea for a Universal History with Cosmopolitan Intent*, 28; *Kleine Schriften*, 35; *Quarrel Among the Faculties*, 64; *Religion within the Bounds of Mere Reason*, 1, 5, 9; transcendental logic, 42, D1812
Kaufmann, Walter, *The Faith of a Heretic*, 18, *From Shakespeare to Existentialism, passim*; *Nietzsche*, 39, 56
Keyserlingk, Hermann von, 55
Kierkegaard, Søren, P, 2, 4, 17, 28, 37, 39, 52, 63, 64, 68, 70, I.2, I.3, II.1, III.1, III.3, IV.2; atti-
tude toward truth and Hegel, III.1; *Concluding Unscientific Postcript*, 63, 68, 70, I.2, I.3; *Edifying Discourses*, I.2; *Fear and Trembling*, 64; *Sickness unto Death*, II.1
Knebel, Karl Ludwig von, 60, D1807*, D1807, D1810*
knowledge vs. love of knowledge, I.1
Knox, T. M., 9, 21, 52, 58
Kojève, Alexandre, 68
Kroner, Richard, *Von Kant bis Hegel*, P
Krug, Wilhelm Traugott, 17, 19, 21, 23, 26, 51, 66; *Allgemeines Handwörterbuch*, 66
Kunstreligion, 8

ladder, *The Phenomenology* as, II.2
Lambert, Johann Heinrich, 35
Lasson, Georg, P, 14, 17, 19–21, 30, 33, 52, 53, 60, I.1, I.2, II.1, III.3, IV.1
Lazarus, Moritz, 35
leap, qualitative, I.3
Leibniz, G. W., 18, 20, 24, 41, 62, 66, 67
Lenin, V. I. U., 68
Lessing, G. E., P, 1, 6, 13, 14, 24, 41, 56, 62, D1795, D1810, III.1
Leutwein, Christian Philipp, 3
Lewes, George Henry, 66
Lichtenberg, Georg Christoph, 30
Lincoln, Abraham, 62
List der Vernunft, 62, III.3
Locke, John, 66, I.1
Loewenberg, J., 29, 33, 52, I.1, III.3
Löffler, Johann Jacob, 4
Logic versus logic, 19
loneliness of philosopher, D1807, D1816
Longinus, 4
Löwith, Karl, *Von Hegel bis Nietzsche*, D1832
Luke 15:16, I.2
Luther, Martin, 5, 7, 8, D1805
Lycon, 4

Macran, H. S., 43
Magna Charta, 62

Malebranche, Nicolas, 66
Mann, Thomas, I.3
Marathon, 63
Marcuse, Herbert, *Reason and Revolution*, 58, Chapter VIII motto
Marx, Karl, 33, 37, 52, 68, 70, I.3, II.2
master and servant, 33
mathematics, III.2
Matthew, cited, IV.3
maturity, stages of, 31, I.1
mauvaise foi, II.1
McTaggart, J. M. E. M., 37, 43, 68
mediaeval philosophy, 66
mediation, 44, II.1, II.3
Meier, Georg Friedrich, 51
Meiner, Felix, 52
Meiners, Christoph, *Briefe über die Schweiz*, D1796
Meinung ist mein, 67
Melitus, 4
Mendelssohn, Moses, 4
metaphysics, Hegel's revolution in, 42
Meyerbeer, G., D1854
mind, III.2. See also *Geist* and spirit
Mitwelt, IV.3
moment or stage, 7, 42, 67, I.1, I.3, II.3
Mommsen, Theodor, III.2
Montesquieu, Baron de, 60, D1870
Moore, G. E., 37, 68
moralische Weltanschauung, 31
Moralität, 3, 5, 6, 7, 10, 21, 37, 63, 64, II.3
moral world order, II.1
Moses, 26
Mozart, Wolfgang Amadeus, 1, 27, D1797
Müller, or Mueller, Gustav E., (different spelling in German and American publications), 4, 19, 24, D1810, Chapter VIII motto, III.3
Mure, G. R. G., P
Murray, Gilbert, 65
myth, 65, 67

Nachwelt, IV.3
Napoleon, 1, 22, 27, 41, D1806, D1814, D1816

nature, D1796, II.3; beauty of, 53; philosophy of, 56, 57
necessary & necessity, 12, 17, I.1, III.3
negative, negativity, 28, II.1, III.1–3
negative and positive philosophy, 68, 70
negative, the power of the, II.3
Nelson, Leonard, III.3
Neoplatonism, 66, III.3
Neoptolemus, 6
New Academy, 66
New York Times Book Review, 1
Nicolin, F., 52
Niebuhr, B. G., D1816
Niemöller, Martin, 28
Niethammer, Friedrich Immanuel, 4, 22, 26, 39–41, D1795, D1805*, D1806*, D1807*, D1808*, D1812*, D1814*, D1816
Nietzsche, Friedrich, 7, 8, 15, 20, 24, 33, 37, 38, 40, 45, 48, 52, 54, 60, 68–70, II.1, III.3
night in which all cows are black, I.3
nobody understood me, 26
non-ego, D1795
nothing, 46, 47
notion, II.3, IV.1. See also *Begriff* and *Vorstellung*
Nous, III.3. See also *Geist*
Novalis (pseudonym of Friedrich von Hardenberg), 1, 25, 35

oak and acorn, I.3
object, II.3, III.1
Occam, William of, 66
Odysseus, 33, 34, 42
Olbers, H. W. M., 15
ontogenetic principle, II.3
ontological argument, 17, 46
opinion, 67
Orff, Carl, D1804
Oriental art, D1835
Origen, 30
originality, 16, D1816
Otto, Rudolf, *Das Heilige*, III.3

painting, D1796
palette with two colors, III.3
Panlogismus, III.3

pantheism, 70
Parmenides, 27, 47
Parthey, G., Report of a Conversation with Goethe, D1827*
passion, 2, I.2
Passmore, John, *A Hundred Years of Philosophy*, 66
Paul, St., 37
Paulus, Caroline, D1808*
Paulus, H. E. G., 4, 14, 53, D1808
Pelczynski, Z. A., 21, 58
Pericles, 62
Pfaffe, Pfaffentum, 5
philosophic disagreement, I.1
philosophical instruction at Gymnasia (detailed discussion), D1812
philosophical instruction at universities (detailed discussion), D1816
philosophical method, III.3
philosophizing vs. philosophy, D1812
philosophizing, natural, IV.2
philosophy, need for, 14
Piazzi, Giuseppe, 15
Pindar, II.1
Plato, 4, 15, 18, 20, 21, 24, 27, 30–32, 34, 37, 42, 47, 59–61, 65, 66, 70, D1835, I.2–3, II.3, III.2, IV.3; *Apology*, 4, 18, 27; *Laws*, IV.1; *Republic*, 31, 61; *Parmenides*, 18, 24, II.3, IV.3; *Symposium*, D1835; *Timaeus*, 15, III.2
Plautus, 4
play theory, Schiller's, 7
Plutarch, III.2
pneuma, 65; see *Geist*, spirit
Pöggeler, Otto, 22, 39, 52
Pope, Alexander, 2
Popper, Karl, *The Open Society and Its Enemies*, 26
positivism, 19
pour soi, II.1
predicate, II.1, IV.1
pre-Socratics, 66
Proclus, III.3, IV.2, IV.3
prodigal son, I.2
progress, D1813
propositions, 7, 19, III.1, IV.1; about God, II.1, IV.1; basic, 14, 19, II.1
Proust, Marcel, 60, I.2

proverbs, IV.2
Prussia, 62, II.1
Psalms, I.2
psychoanalysis, III.3
Ptolemy I, IV.2
Pyrrho, 18, 19
Pythagoreans, 21
Pythagorean theorem, III.2

Raphael, 14
räsonnieren, IV.1
rational procedure, 37
Raumer, Friedrich Ludwig Georg von, D1816*
reason, see understanding
reflection, I.2, II.1
Reformation, 20
refutation, II.1
Reinhold, Karl Leonhard, 14
Reizenstein, Sigmund Karl Johann von, D1805
religion, folk, 8, 9, 21; to be feared, D1807
Rembrandt, II.3
Renaissance philosophy, 66
Renan, Ernest, 9
Restoration, 1
result, naked, I.1, II.1
retreat into essence, III.2
Rickert, Heinrich, 68
Riemer, Friedrich Wilhelm, D1810
Riesman, David, 64
Rilke, R. M., 28
Ritter, Heinrich Julius, 54
Roos, Carl, 68
Rosenkranz, Karl, 3, 4, 10, 15, 18, 21, 23, 24, 30, 39, 40, 51, 53, 55, 66, D1844*
Rosenzweig, Franz, *Hegel und der Staat*, P, 11, 40, 58
Ross, W. D., III.3
Rossini, G. A., 1
Roth, Karl Johann Friedrich, D1816
Rousseau, Jean Jacques, 3
royal road, IV.2
Royce, Josiah, P, 13, 29, 33, 37, 38, 68, D1806, I.3, III.3
Russell, Bertrand, 37; *History of Western Philosophy*, 67
Ryle, Gilbert, *The Concept of Mind*, 34, 67

Sache, I.1, III.3

Sartre, Jean-Paul, P, 33, 35, 60, 64, 68, I.2, II.1

Schadenfreude, 15

Scheler, Max, 35

Schelling, Friedrich Wilhelm Joseph von, P, 1, 3, 4, 5, 7, 10, 14, 16, 18, 21–27, 30, 37, 39, 41, 54, 56, 58, 66, 68, 70, D1795*, D1796*, D1802*, D1803*, D1804*, D1807*, D1808*, D1812, D1816, D1829*, I.2, I.3, II.1, III.3; quotations, I.3

Schelling, Caroline, D1802, D1829*

Schema, Schemen, III.3

schematism, 53

Schiller, Friedrich von, P, 1, 2, 3, 5, 10, 12, 14, 16, 20, 21, 23, 24, 26, 34, 51, 62, 65, I.2, II.3, D1795, D1798*, D1799, D1805; *Letters on the Aesthetic Education of Man,* P, 3, 7, 8, 10, 12, 16, I.2

Schlegel, A. W., D1802

Schlegel, Caroline, D1802

Schlegel, Friedrich von, 1, 25, 26, D1807, D1816, I.2, I.3

Schleiermacher, Friedrich Ernst Daniel, 1, 54, 55, 62, D1819*, I.2

scholasticism, 66, II.3

Schopenhauer, Arthur, 4, 24, 34, 54, 62; on mathematics, III.2

Schuckmann, Kaspar, Friedrich Freiherr von, D1816*

Schulze, Gottlob Ernst, 18, 19, 21, 26, 51

Schwärmerei, I.2

science, elevation of philosophy to a, 16, 37, I.1

Seckendorf, *Taschenbuch,* D1807

Seebeck, Thomas Johann, D1807

selbstbewusst, 33

selbstisch, III.1

sensibility, II.3

Sermon on the Mount, 8, 10

Sextus Empiricus, 19, II.2

Shakespeare, William, 14, 34, 41, 48, 60; *Merry Wives,* D1832 (1st item in D)

Sinclair, Isaak von, D1804, D1807*

Sittlichkeit, 3, 6, 7, 10, 21 (detailed explanation), 30, 35, 37, 57, 58, 63–65, II.3

skepticism, 18–19, 28, 33, 66

sleep, wisdom in, I.2

Smith, John E., 29

Socrates, 4, 8, 15, 18, 64, 66, D1795, D1835, II.3

Solger, Karl Wilhelm Ferdinand, 53

Soll, Ivan, 33

Solon, 30

Sophists, 27, 66

Sophocles, 4, 6, 7, 13, 14, 21, 28, 30–32, 36, 60, 64, 65, D1804; *Antigone,* 4, 6, 7, 13, 30–32, 36, 64, 65; *Oedipus at Colonus,* 4, 30; *Philoctetes,* 6

space, III.2

Spengler, Oswald, 60

Spieltrieb, 7

Spinoza, B. de, 14, 20, 21, 24, 25, 65, 66, 70, D1795, D1816, D1870, I.1, II.1, III.3; *determinatio negatio est,* II.1

spirit, 7, 22, 24, 34, 65, I.2, I.3, II.1

spirit, absolute as, 57, II.1

Spirit, Holy, 34, III.1

spirit, objective, 57; strength only as great as expression, I.2; subjective, 57

spirit versus letter, 7, 26, D1795

spirit, world, 65, II.2, II.3

Stace, W. T., *The Philosophy of Hegel,* P, 43, 57

stages, educational, II.3. See also moment

state, 21, 58, 63

Stewart, Dugald, 66

Stirling, J. Hutchison, *The Secret of Hegel,* 24

Stoicism, 28, 33, 66

Strauss, David Friedrich, 9, 31, 38, 66, D1797, D1831*

Ströhlin, Friedrich Jakob, D1803

Strömer von Reichenbach auf Holenstein, Helena Maria Katharina Karoline (daughter) and Maria Sabina Hedwig Freifrau von (mother), D1810

style, speculative versus argumentative, IV.1

subject, II.3, III.1, III.3; vs. sub-stance, II.1
subject matter, I.1
sublimate, 7, 12, 34, 42, II.1, II.3, III.1, IV.1
substance, D1795, II.1, III.3
Suetonius, III.2
supposed to suppose, IV.1
Suthmeier, Hermann, 18
synthesis, see antithesis
system, 14, 16, Chapter V, D1816, I.1, II.1

Tacitus, 4
teleology, II.1
theodicy, 62, D1807
theology, 62, D1795, D1840
theoretical work accomplishes more than practical work, D1808
Thersites, 60
thesis, see antithesis
thing in itself, 42, IV.1
thinking for oneself, D1816
thinking, argumentative, IV.1; rep-resentational, IV.1; thinking that comprehends, IV.1
Thorwaldsen, Bertel, 53
Thucydides, 4, 27
Tieck, Ludwig, D1807
Tillich, Paul, 39, 65, I.2, IV.1
time, III.2
time of birth and transition, I.3
tollere, 42
tradition-directedness, 64
tragedy, D1814. See also Sopho-cles, etc.
triads, 40, 53, III.3. See also dia-lectic
triangle, III.2
triplicity, 40, 53, III.3. See also dialectic
true & false, III.1
truth prevails when its time has come, IV.3
truths, mathematical vs. historical, accidental, arbitrary, III.2
Tucker, Robert, 33
Tyrtaeus, 4

übersieht, III.3
Ueberweg, Geschichte der Philo-sophie, 31, 33

understanding as the absolute power, II.3; tabular, III.3; ver-sus reason, 7, 14, 16, 18–20, 42
unfamiliar, III.3
unhappy consciousness, 32, 33, I.2
United States, 1
U. S. Constitution, 63; fifth amendment, 64
Unmittelbarkeit, 44, I.3
unmoved mover, II.1

Van Gogh, Vincent, 69
Van Paassen, Pierre, Why Jesus Died, 9
verkehrt, 16, II.2, III.2
Virgil, 4, 14
void, the, III.1
Voigt, Christian Gottlob von, D1807
Voltaire, Arouet François Marie, Candide, 41
Vorbegriff, 19
Vorländer, Karl, 7
Vorstellung, 34, 65, I.2
Voss, Johann Heinrich, D1805*

Wagner, Richard, 30, 65, IV.2
Wallace, William, P, 52
Waterloo, 1
Weber, Max, Wissenschaft als Beruf, 37, III.3
Wechselwirkung, 14
Weltgeist, 65, II.2, II.3
Whitehead, Modes of Thought, quoted, 37
Whitman, Walt, D1881*
whole, the true is the, II.1
Winckelmann, J. J., 6
Windelband, Wilhelm, 68
Windischmann, Karl Josef Hier-onymus, 39, D1808*, D1809*, D1810*; review of Phenomenol-ogy in Jenaer Allgemeine Literatur-Zeitung, D1809*
Wirklickkeit, I.3
Wittgenstein, Ludwig, Philosophi-cal Investigations, 21; Tractatus Logico-Philosophicus, II.2
Wolf, Christian, 66
world-historical individuals and peoples, 62, 64
world soul, D1806
world spirit, 65, II.2, II.3

Xenophanes, 18

Zeller, Eduard, 68
Zellmann, Christian Gotthold, D1807*
Zelter, Karl Friedrich, Goethe's correspondence with, P, D1831*, D1832*
Zeno of Elea, 18, 37
Zerrissenheit, II.3
Zeus, IV.2

Acknowledgments

For over a dozen years I have taught Hegel both in graduate seminars and to undergraduates. I want to give thanks to my graduate students for their interest and helpful discussions, above all to Professor Frithjof Bergmann who wrote his thesis on Hegel. In the spring of 1964, Ivan Soll checked my translation of the preface to the *Phenomenology* against the German original, and Richard Schacht and Charles Love compared it with Baillie's version. Much of the work on the Index was done by Michael Spence. I am grateful to Sanford G. Thatcher for his cheerful and reliable help with the proofs and other last-minute chores.

My debts to scholars are acknowledged throughout the book. But I should like to add that one of my teachers, Professor John William Miller of Williams College, who never lectured on Hegel, often remarked that Hegel's philosophy was much more open and less rigid than is usually supposed. I am most indebted to Georg Lasson, who pioneered the critical editions of Hegel's writings, to Johannes Hoffmeister, who continued this work and edited Hegel's letters—he also had my first article on Hegel translated and published in Germany— and to Rolf Flechsig, who edited the fourth volume of Hegel's correspondence after Hoffmeister's death. All Hegel scholars have reason to be grateful to Felix Meiner who, for over half a century, has published these critical editions.

For his companionship during the hours before and after midnight when much of this book was written during the summer of 1964, I thank my son, David. My debt to my wife,

Hazel, is chronic by now. And thanks to Anne Freedgood and Robert Hewetson, the final stages, after the manuscript was turned over to the publisher, were free from birth pangs: one could not wish for more understanding editors.

ANCHOR BOOKS

PHILOSOPHY

AFRICAN RELIGIONS AND PHILOSOPHY—John S. Mbiti, A754

THE ALIENATION OF REASON: A History of Positivist Thought—Leszek Kolakowski; Norbert Guterman, A661

THE AMERICAN TRANSCENDENTALISTS—Perry Miller, ed., A119

AQUINAS: A Collection of Critical Essays—Anthony Kenny, ed., AP8

BASIC WRITINGS ON POLITICS AND PHILOSOPHY—Karl Marx and Friedrich Engels; Lewis S. Feuer, eds., A185

THE BIRTH OF TRAGEDY and THE GENEALOGY OF MORALS—Friedrich Nietzsche; Francis Golffing, trans., A81

BODY AND MIND—Keith Campbell, PP2

THE BROKEN IMAGE: Man, Science and Society—Floyd Matson, A506

COMEDY, "Laughter"—Henri Bergson—"Essay on Comedy" by George Meredith; intro. and supplementary essay by Wylie Sypher, A87

THE COSMOLOGICAL ARGUMENTS: A Spectrum of Opinion—Donald R. Burrill, ed., A586

CRITICAL EXISTENTIALISM—Nicola Abbagnano; Nino Langiulli, trans. and ed., A642

CRITIQUE OF PURE REASON—Immanuel Kant: F. Max Muller, trans., A551

CRITIQUE OF RELIGION AND PHILOSOPHY—Walter Kaufmann, A252

CUSTOM, LAW, AND MORALITY: Conflict and Continuity in Social Behavior—Burton M. Leiser, A669

DESCARTES: A Collection of Critical Essays—Willis Doney, ed., AP5

EITHER/OR, Volume I—Søren Kierkegaard; David F. Swenson and Lillian Marven Swenson, trans., revised with a Foreward by Howard A. Johnson, A181a

EITHER/OR, Volume II—Søren Kierkegaard; Walter Lowrie, trans., revised with a Foreword by Howard A. Johnson, A181b

ESSAYS IN PHILOSOPHICAL PSYCHOLOGY—Donald F. Gustafson, ed., A417

ETHICAL IMPERATIVE—Richard Means, A735

ETHICS AND SOCIETY—Richard T. de George, ed., A512

EVANGELICAL THEOLOGY—Karl Barth, A408

EVOLUTION AND CHRISTIAN HOPE—Ernst Benz, A607

THE FAITH OF A HERETIC—Walter Kaufmann, A336

FIVE STAGES OF GREEK RELIGION—Gilbert Murray, A51

FOUR EXISTENTIALIST THEOLOGIANS: A Reader from the Work of Jacques Maritain, Nicholas Berdyaev, Martin Buber, and Paul Tillich—Will Herberg, ed., A141

FREUD: The Mind of the Moralist—Philip Rieff, A278

FROM HEGEL TO NIETZSCHE: The Revolution in Nineteenth Century Thought—Karl Lowith; David E. Green, trans., A553

FROM SHAKESPEARE TO EXISTENTIALISM—Walter Kaufmann, A213

FROM STONE AGE TO CHRISTIANITY—W. F. Albright, A100

GUILT: Man and Society—Roger W. Smith, ed., A768

HEGEL: A Reinterpretation—Walter Kaufmann, A528a

HEGEL: Texts and Commentary—Walter Kaufmann, ed. and trans., A528b

HUME: A Collection of Critical Essays—V. C. Chappell, ed., AP2

INDIVIDUALS: An Essay in Descriptive Metaphysics—P. F. Strawson, A364

AN INTRODUCTION TO ETHICS—J. D. Mabbott, A662

AN INTRODUCTION TO LOGIC—David Mitchell, A714

AN INTRODUCTION TO METAPHYSICS—Martin Heidegger; Ralph Manheim, trans., A251

IRRATIONAL MAN—William Barrett, A351

KANT: A Collection of Critical Essays—Robert Paul Wolff, ed., AP4

LOGIC AND LANGUAGE, First and Second Series—A. G. N. Flew, ed., A449

MAIN CURRENTS IN SOCIOLOGICAL THOUGHT, Volume I: Montesquieu, Comte, Marx, Tocqueville, the Sociologists and the Revolution of 1848—Raymond Aron; Richard Howard and Helen Weaver, trans., A600a

MAIN CURRENTS IN SOCIOLOGICAL THOUGHT, Volume II: Durkheim, Pareto, Weber—Raymond Aron, A600b

MAN IN THE MODERN AGE—Karl Jaspers; Eden and Cedar Paul, trans., A101

MARTIN LUTHER: Selections from His Writings—John Dillenberger, ed., A271

MARX IN THE MID-TWENTIETH CENTURY—Gajo Petrović, A584

MARXISM AND EXISTENTIALISM—Walter Odajnyx, A443

THE MARXISM OF JEAN-PAUL SARTRE—Wilfrid Desan, A507

MEMORY—Don Locke, PP3

THE METAPHYSICAL FOUNDATIONS OF MODERN SCIENCE—E. A. Burtt, A41

MILL: A Collection of Critical Essays—J. B. Scheewind, ed., AP7

MODERN DEDUCTIVE LOGIC—Robert J. Ackermann, NP1

MODERN MORAL PHILOSOPHY—W. D. Hudson, NP2

MODERN SCIENCE AND MODERN MAN—James B. Conant, A10

THE OCHRE ROBE—Agehananda Bharati, A776

THE ONTOLOGICAL ARGUMENT FROM ST. ANSELM TO CONTEMPORARY PHILOSOPHERS—Alvin Plantinga, ed., intro. by Richard Taylor, A435

PATTERNS OF ANARCHY: A Collection of Writings on the Anarchist Tradition—Leonard I. Krimerman and Lewis Parry, eds., A501

PERCEIVING, SENSING, AND KNOWING: A Book of Readings from Twentieth-Century Sources on the Philosophy of Perception—Robert J. Swartz, ed., A460

PHENOMENOLOGY: The Philosophy of Edmund Husserl and Its Interpretation—Joseph J. Kockelmans, ed., A585

THE PHILOSOPHY OF HISTORY IN OUR TIME—Hans Meyerhoff, ed., A164

THE PHILOSOPHY OF SOCRATES—Gregory Vlastos, ed., AP11

PRAGMATIC PHILOSOPHY—Amelie Rorty, ed., A538

PSYCHE AND SYMBOL—C. G. Jung, A136

RYLE: A Collection of Critical Essays—Oscar P. Wood and George Pitcher, eds., AP10

SELECTIONS FROM THE WRITINGS OF KIERKEGAARD—Lee M. Hollander, trans., revised edition, A210

SOCIAL AND POLITICAL PHILOSOPHY: Readings from Plato to Gandhi—John Somerville and Ronald Santoni, eds., A370

SOCIALIST HUMANISM: An International Symposium—Erich Fromm, ed., A529

SOCRATES: The Man and His Thought—A. E. Taylor, A9

STRUCTURALISM—Jacques Ehrmann, ed., A719

THE SUFIS—Idries Shah, A765

THE TACIT DIMENSION—Michael Polanyi, A540

THE TANTRIC TRADITION—Agehananda Bharati, A745

THE THEORY OF KNOWLEDGE—D. W. Hamlyn, NP3

THE THREE JEWELS: An Introduction to Modern Buddhism—Bhikshu Sangharakshita (Stavira), A763

THREE WAYS OF THOUGHT IN ANCIENT CHINA—Arthur Waley, A75

TRAGEDY AND PHILOSOPHY—Walter Kaufmann, A689

TRUTH—Alan R. White, PP1

UNIVERSALS AND PARTICULARS: Readings in Ontology—Michael J. Loux, ed., A722

WITTGENSTEIN: The Philosophical Investigations—A Collection of Critical Essays—George Pitcher, ed., AP3

WORLD OF THE BUDDHA: A Reader—From the Three Baskets to Modern Zen—Lucien Stryk, ed., A615

WRITINGS OF THE YOUNG MARX ON PHILOSOPHY AND SOCIETY—Loyd D. Easton and Kurt H. Guddat, trans. and eds., A583

ZEN: Poems, Prayers, Sermons, Anecdotes, Interviews—Lucien Stryk and Takashi Ikemoto, eds. and trans., A485

ZEN BUDDHISM: Selected Writings of D. T. Suzuki—William Barrett, ed., A90

ZEN FLESH, ZEN BONES: A Collection of Zen and Pre-Zen Writings—Paul Reps, ed., A233

ANCHOR BOOKS

HISTORY

AFRICA AND THE VICTORIANS—Ronald Robinson and John Gallagher, with Alice Denny, AO4

AGAINST THE WORLD: Attitudes of White South Africa—Douglas Brown, A671

THE AGE OF COURTS AND KINGS: Manners and Morals 1588–1715—Philippe Erlanger, A691

THE AGE OF GEORGE III—R. J. White, A706

AGRARIAN PROBLEMS AND PEASANT MOVEMENTS IN LATIN AMERICA—Rodolfo Stavenhagen, ed., A718

THE ANCIENT CITY—Fustel de Coulanges, A76

ANTIWORLDS AND "THE FIFTH AGE"—Andrei Voznesensky; Patricia Blake and Max Hayward, eds., bilingual edition, A595

THE ARAB WORLD TODAY—Morroe Berger, A406

BACK OF HISTORY, The Story of Our Origins—William Howells, revised edition, N34

BASIC WRITINGS ON POLITICS AND PHILOSOPHY—Karl Marx and Friedrich Engels; Lewis S. Feuer, ed., A185

THE BIBLE FOR STUDENTS OF LITERATURE AND ART—G. B. Harrison, ed., A394

THE BIBLICAL ARCHAEOLOGIST READER, Volume III—Edward F. Campbell, Jr. and David Noel Freedman, eds., A250c

BIRTH OF CIVILIZATION IN THE NEAR EAST—Henri Frankfort, A89

THE BOOK OF THE COURTIER—Baldesar Castiglione; Charles S. Singleton, trans., Edgar de N. Mayhew, ill. ed., A186

BRATSK STATION AND OTHER NEW POEMS, Yevgeny Yevtushenko—Tina Tupikina Glaessner, Geoffrey Dutton and Igor Mezhakoff-Koriakin, trans., intro. by Rosh Ireland, A558

CHOU EN-LAI—Kai-Yu Hsu, A652

CRISIS IN EUROPE: 1580–1660—Trevor Aston, ed., intro. by Christopher Hill, A575

DARWIN, MARX, WAGNER: Critique of a Heritage—Jacques Barzun, revised second edition, A127

THE DEAD SEA SCRIPTURES—Theodore Gaster, trans., revised and enlarged, A378

DEMOCRACY VERSUS EMPIRE: The Jamaica Riots of 1865 and the Governor Eyre Controversy—Bernard Semmel, A703

DISCOVERIES AND OPINIONS OF GALILEO—Stillman Drake, trans., A94

THE DISCOVERY OF INDIA—Jawaharlal Nehru; Robert I. Crane, ed., abridged, A200

EAGLES IN COBWEBS: Nationalism and Communism in the Balkans—Paul Lendvai, A687

EARLY MAN IN THE NEW WORLD—Kenneth MacGowan and Joseph A. Hester, Jr., revised edition, N22

THE EASTERN ORTHODOX CHURCH—Ernest Benz, A332

1848: The Revolution of the Intellectuals—Lewis Namier, A385
9Ab

THE END OF THE JEWISH PEOPLE?—Georges Friedmann; Eric Mosbacher, trans., A626

ENGLAND: Prehistory to the Present—Arvel B. Erickson and Martin J. Havran, AO2

ENVY AND OTHER WORKS—Yuro Olesha; Andrew R. MacAndrew, trans., A571

ESSAYS ON OLD TESTAMENT HISTORY AND RELIGION—Albrecht Alt; R. A. Wilson, trans., A544

EUROPEAN DIPLOMATIC HISTORY 1789–1815: France Against Europe—Steven T. Ross, A645

THE FACE OF THE ANCIENT ORIENT—Sabatino Moscati, A289

FIVE STAGES OF GREEK RELIGIONS—Gilbert Murray, A51

FOUR STAGES OF RENAISSANCE STYLE—Wylie Sypher, A44

FROM FERTILITY CULT TO WORSHIP: A Reassessment for the Modern Church of the Worship of Ancient Israel—Walter Harrelson, A713

FROM HEGEL TO NIETZSCHE—Karl Lowith; David E. Green, trans., A553

FROM THE STONE AGE TO CHRISTIANITY: Monotheism and the Historical Process—William Foxwell Albright, A100

THE GATEWAY TO HISTORY—Allan Nevins, revised edition, A314

GOOD-BYE TO ALL THAT—Robert Graves, revised second edition, A123

GUESTS OF THE SHEIK: The Ethnography of an Iraqi Village—Elizabeth Warnock Fernea, A693

HALF-WAY TO THE MOON: New Writing from Russia—Patricia Blake and Max Hayward, A483

A HERO OF OUR TIME—Mihail Lermontov; Vladimir Nabokov and Dmitri Nabokov, trans., A133

HISTORY AND SOCIAL THEORY—Gordon Leff, A781

HISTORY BEGINS AT SUMER—Samuel Noah Kramer, A175

A HISTORY OF EAST AND CENTRAL AFRICA: To the Late Nineteenth Century—Basil Davidson, A677

HISTORY OF ENGLAND: In Three Volumes—G. M. Trevelyan, A22a, b, and c

A HISTORY OF EUROPE: Two Volumes—Henri Pirenne, A156a, b

A HISTORY OF ROME from its origins to 529 A.D. as Told by the Roman Historians—Moses Hadas, ed., A78

A HISTORY OF WEST AFRICA—Basil Davidson, with F. K. Buah and the advice of J. F. Ade Ajayi, A550

HITLER'S SOCIAL REVOLUTION—David Schoenbaum, A590

HOW THE GREEKS BUILT CITIES—R. E. Wycherley, A674

THE IMPERIAL IDEA AND ITS ENEMIES—A. P. Thornton, A627

IMPERIALISM AND SOCIAL REFORM: English Social-Imperial Thought 1895–1914—Bernard Semmel, A618

ISLAM—Fazlur Rahman, A641

ITALY FROM THE RISORGIMENTO TO FASCISM—A. William Salomone, ed., A737

JOHN CALVIN: Selections from His Writings—John Dillenberger, ed., A751

JOURNEYS TO ENGLAND AND IRELAND—Alexis de Tocqueville; J. P. Mayer, ed., A611

KARL MARX ON COLONIALISM AND MODERNIZATION—Shlomo Avineri, ed., A688

THE LAND TO THOSE WHO WORK IT: Algeria's Experiment in Worker Management—Thomas L. Blair, A734

LATIN AMERICAN POLITICS: Studies of the Contemporary Scene—Robert D. Tomasek, ed., new revised and updated edition, A498

LIFE IN MEXICO: The Letters of Fanny Calderón de la Barca with New Material from the Author's Private Journals—Howard J. Fisher and Marion Hall Fisher, eds., AO16

A MAN OF THE PEOPLE—Chinua Achebe, A594

MAO TSE-TUNG ON REVOLUTION AND WAR—Mostafa Rehai, ed., A730

MARX IN THE MID-TWENTIETH CENTURY: A Yugoslav Philosopher Reconsiders Karl Marx's Writings—Gajo Petrović, A584

THE MIND OF THE EUROPEAN ROMANTICS—H. G. Schenk, A655

MONT-SAINT-MICHEL AND CHARTRES—Henry Adams, A166

MOTHER EARTH AND OTHER STORIES—Boris Pilnyak; Vera T. Reck and Michael Green, trans. and eds., A625

MYTHOLOGIES OF THE ANCIENT WORLD—Samuel Noah Kramer, ed., A229

THE NAZI REVOLUTION 1933-35: Prelude to Calamity—Eliot Barculo Wheaton, A690

NEW DIRECTIONS IN BIBLICAL ARCHAEOLOGY—David Noel Freedman and Jonas C. Greenfield, eds., A753

A NEW HISTORY OF THE COLD WAR—John Lukacs, third edition, expanded, of A History of the Cold War, A533

NOBODY WANTED WAR: Misperception in Vietnam and Other Wars—Ralph K. White, A612

OBSTACLES TO DEVELOPMENT IN LATIN AMERICA—Celso Furtado, A747

THE OLD REGIME AND THE FRENCH REVOLUTION—Alexis de Tocqueville; Stuart Gilbert, trans., A60

THE PACIFIC ISLANDS—Douglas L. Oliver, revised edition, N14

THE PATH TO DICTATORSHIP, 1918-1933: Ten Essays by German Scholars—John Conway, trans.; intro. by Fritz Stern, A547

THE PHILOSOPHY OF HISTORY IN OUR TIME—Hans Meyerhoff, ed., A164

THE POLITICS OF CULTURAL DESPAIR—Fritz Stern, A436

POOR PEOPLE and A LITTLE HERO—Fyodor Dostoevsky; David Magarshack, trans., A619

QUEEN ELIZABETH I—J. E. Neale, A105

RECOLLECTIONS—Alexis de Tocqueville; J. P. Mayer and A. P. Kerr, eds., A749

THE RECORDS OF MEDIEVAL EUROPE—Carolly Erickson, ed., A770
9Cb

THE RELIGIONS OF MANKIND—Hans-Joachim Schoeps; Richard and Clara Winston, trans., A621

REVOLUTIONARY RUSSIA—Richard Pipes, ed., A685

RETURN TO LAUGHTER—Elenore Smith Bowen, Foreword by David Riesman, N36

THE RUSSIAN REVOLUTION: The Overthrow of Tzarism and the Triumph of the Soviets—Leon Trotsky: F. W. Dupee, ed., selected from The History of the Russian Revolution, Max Eastman, trans., A170

SCIENCE AND CIVIC LIFE IN THE ITALIAN RENAISSANCE—Eugenio Garin; Peter Munz, trans., A647

THE SEVENTEENTH-CENTURY BACKGROUND—Basil Willey, A19

A SHORT HISTORY OF SCIENCE: Origins and Results of the Scientific Revolution—Herbert Butterfield and Others, A180

SOCIALIST THOUGHT—Albert Fried and Ronald Sanders, eds., A384

SOCIETY AND DEMOCRACY IN GERMANY—Ralf Dahrendorf, A684

SOCRATES—A. E. Taylor, A9

THE SOUTHEAST ASIAN WORLD—Keith Buchanan, A639

THE SPLENDID CENTURY: Life in the France of Louis XIV—W. H. Lewis, A122

STUDIES OF LATIN AMERICAN SOCIETIES—T. Lynn Smith, A702

THE THIRTY YEARS WAR—C. V. Wedgwood, A249

THREE SHORT NOVELS OF DOSTOEVSKY—Constance Garnett, trans.; Avrahm Yarmolinsky, ed. and revised, A193

THREE WAYS OF THOUGHT IN ANCIENT CHINA—Arthur Waley, A75

TODAY'S LATIN AMERICA—Robert J. Alexander, second edition, revised, A327

TO THE FINLAND STATION: A Study in the Writing and Acting of History—Edmund Wilson, A6

THE TOWN LABOURER: The New Civilization 1760–1832—J. L. and Barbara Hammond, Preface by Asa Briggs, A632

THE TRIUMPH OF THE MIDDLE CLASSES—Charles Morazé, A633

VIETNAM: THE ORIGINS OF REVOLUTION—John T. McAlister, Jr., A761

THE VILLAGE OF VIRIATINO: An Ethnographic Study of a Russian Village from Before the Revolution to the Present—Sula Benet, trans. and ed., A758

THE WANING OF THE MIDDLE AGES—J. Huizanga, A42

WHITE MAN, LISTEN!—Richard Wright, A414

WRITINGS OF THE YOUNG MARX ON PHILOSOPHY AND SOCIETY—Loyd D. Easton and Kurt H. Guddat, trans. and ed., A583

A YEAR IS EIGHT MONTHS: Czechoslovakia 1968—Journalist M, A750

ANCHOR BOOKS

POLITICAL SCIENCE AND GOVERNMENT

AFRICA AND THE VICTORIANS: The Climax of Imperialism—Ronal Robinson and John Gallagher, A614

AGRARIAN PROBLEMS AND PEASANT MOVEMENTS IN LATIN AMERICA—Rodolfo Stavenhagen, ed., A718

ANATOMY OF A METROPOLIS—Edgar M. Hoover and Raymon Vernon, A298

AND WE ARE NOT SAVED: A History of the Movement as People—Debbie Louis, A755

THE ARAB WORLD TODAY—Morroe Berger, A406

ARROW OF GOD—Chinua Achebe, intro. by K. W. J. Post, A698

BASIC WRITINGS ON POLITICS AND PHILOSOPHY—Karl Marx and Friedrich Engels: Lewis S. Feuer, ed., A185

BLACK AWAKENING IN CAPITALIST AMERICA—Robert L. Allen, A759

CHEMICAL AND BIOLOGICAL WARFARE: America's Hidden Arsenal—Seymour M. Hersh, A673

THE CIVIL WAR IN AMERICA—Alan Barker, A274

COLD WAR ESSAYS—Gar Alperovitz, intro. by Christopher Lasch A664

COMPARATIVE GOVERNMENT: A Reader—J. Blondel, ed., A681

CONGRESS: The First Branch of Government—Alfred de Grazia ed., slightly abridged, A582

THE CONGRESSMAN: His Work as He Sees It—Charles L. Clapp A426

THE CONTEMPT POWER—Ronald Goldfarb, A777

CUSTOM, LAW, AND MORALITY: Conflict and Continuity in Social Behavior—Burton M. Leiser, A669

THE DEATH PENALTY IN AMERICA—Hugo Adam Bedau, ed., revised edition, A387

THE DEVELOPMENT OF POLITICAL ATTITUDES IN CHILDREN—Robert D. Hess and Judith V. Torney, A640

THE DISCOVERY OF INDIA—Jawaharlal Nehru; Robert I. Crane, ed abridged, A200

A DISSENTER'S GUIDE TO FOREIGN POLICY—Irving Howe, ed., Foreword by Lewis Coser, A617

EAGLES IN COBWEBS: Nationalism and Communism in the Balkan—Paul Lendvai, A687

1848: The Revolution of the Intellectuals—Lewis Namier, A385

THE EMERGING REPUBLICAN MAJORITY—Kevin P. Phillips, AO18

EQUALITY BY STATUTE: The Revolution in Civil Rights—Morroe Berger, A591

THE FEDERALIST PAPERS, Second Edition—Roy P. Fairfield, ed A239

THE FIRST NEW NATION: The United States in Historical and Comparative Perspective—Seymour Martin Lipset, A597

FROM RACE RIOT TO SIT-IN—Arthur Waskow, A557

SAb

THE FUTURE OF CONSERVATISM—M. Stanton Evans, revised edition, A701

GOVERNING EDUCATION: A Reader on Politics, Power and Public School Policy—Alan Rosenthal, ed., A651

IMPERIALISM AND SOCIAL REFORM: English Social-Imperial Thought 1895–1914—Bernard Semmel, A618

THE JEFFERSONIAN AND HAMILTONIAN TRADITIONS IN AMERICAN POLITICS: A Documentary History—Albert Fried, ed., A464

KARL MARX ON COLONIALISM AND MODERNIZATION: His Dispatches and Other Writings on China, India, Mexico, the Middle East and North Africa—Schlomo Avineri, ed., A688

THE LAST LANDSCAPE—William H. Whyte, A717

LATIN AMERICAN POLITICS: Studies of the Contemporary Scene—Robert D. Tomasek, ed., A498

LAW AND PSYCHOLOGY IN CONFLICT—James Marshall, A654

LET THEM EAT PROMISES: The Politics of Hunger in America—Nick Kotz; intro. by Senator George S. McGovern, A788

MAIN CURRENTS IN SOCIOLOGICAL THOUGHT, Volume I: Montesquieu, Comte, Marx, Tocqueville, the Sociologists and the Revolution of 1848—Raymond Aron; Richard Howard and Helen Weaver, trans., A600a

MAIN CURRENTS IN SOCIOLOGICAL THOUGHT, Volume II: Durkheim, Pareto, Weber—Raymond Aron, A600b

A MAN OF THE PEOPLE—Chinua Achebe, A594

MAO TSE-TUNG ON REVOLUTION AND WAR—Mostafa Rejai, ed., A730

MARX AND THE INTELLECTUALS: A Set of Post-Ideological Essays—Lewis Feuer, A643

MARX IN THE MID-TWENTIETH CENTURY: A Yugoslav Philosopher Reconsiders K. Marx's Writings—Galo Petrović, A584

MAX WEBER: An Intellectual Portrait—Reinhard Bendix, A281

MAY MAN PREVAIL?—Erich Fromm, A275

MIRAGE OF HEALTH—René Dubos, A258

MOVEMENT AND REVOLUTION: A Conversation on American Radicalism—Peter L. Berger and Richard J. Neuhaus, A726

THE NAZI REVOLUTION 1933–35: Prelude to Calamity—Eliot Barculo Wheaton, A690

THE NEGRO AND THE AMERICAN LABOR MOVEMENT—Julius Jacobson, ed., A495

THE NEWCOMERS—Oscar Handlin, A283

A NEW HISTORY OF THE COLD WAR—John Lukacs, third edition, expanded, of A History of the Cold War, A533

NOBODY WANTED WAR: Misperception in Vietnam and Other Wars—Ralph K. White, revised and expanded, A612

THE OLD REGIME AND THE FRENCH REVOLUTION—Alexis de Tocqueville; Stuart Gilbert, trans., A60

ON INTELLECTUALS—Philip Rieff, ed., A733

THE PATH TO DICTATORSHIP, 1918–1933, Ten Essays by German Scholars—John Conway, trans., intro. by Fritz Stern, A547

PATTERNS OF ANARCHY: A Collection of Writings on the Anarchis Tradition—Leonard I. Krimerman and Lewis Perry, eds., A501

POLITICAL MAN: The Social Bases of Politics—Seymour Martin Lip set, A330

THE POLITICS OF SCHOOL DESEGREGATION—Robert L. Crain, A665

THE PRESIDENTS' MEN—Patrick Anderson, A705

RACE AND NATIONALITY IN AMERICAN LIFE—Oscar Handlin, A110

THE RADICAL PAPERS—Irving Howe, ed., A532

THE RADICAL RIGHT—Daniel Bell, ed., A376

RECOLLECTIONS—Alexis de Tocqueville; J. P. Mayer and A. P. Kerr eds., A749

THE RELEVANCE OF INTERNATIONAL LAW—Karl Deutsch and Stanley Hoffman, eds., A785

THE RELIGIOUS FACTOR—Gerhard Lenski, A337

REVOLUTION AND COUNTERREVOLUTION: Change and Persistence in Social Structure—Seymour Martin Lipset, A764

REVOLUTIONARY NONVIOLENCE—David Dellinger, A787

REVOLUTIONARY RUSSIA—Richard Pipes, ed., A685

SELECTED WRITINGS OF PIERRE-JOSEPH PROUDHON—Stewart Ed wards, ed.; Elizabeth Fraser, trans., A709

SOCIAL AND POLITICAL PHILOSOPHY: Readings from Plato to Gandhi —John Somerville and Ronald Santoni, eds., A370

SOCIALISM IN AMERICA: From the Shakers to the Third Internationa —Albert Fried, ed., AO15

SOCIALIST HUMANISM: An International Symposium—Erich Fromm ed., A529

SOCIALIST THOUGHT: A Documentary History—Albert Fried and Ronald Sanders, eds., A384

THE SOUTHEAST ASIAN WORLD—Keith Buchanan, A639

TAMING MEGALOPOLIS, Two Volumes—H. Wentworth Eldredge ed., A593a, b

TODAY'S LATIN AMERICA—Robert J. Alexander, second edition re vised, A327

THE TOOLS OF SOCIAL SCIENCE—John Madge, A437

TO THE FINLAND STATION: A Study in the Writing and Acting o History—Edmund Wilson, A6

THE TROUBLED PARTNERSHIP: A Re-appraisal of the Atlantic Alli ance—Henry A. Kissinger, A511

UNION DEMOCRACY—Seymour Martin Lipset, Martin A. Trow, an James S. Coleman, Foreword by Clark Kerr, A296

THE URBAN COMPLEX—Robert C. Weaver, A505

URBAN RENEWAL: People, Politics and Planning—Jewel Bellush an Murray Hausknecht, eds., A569

VIETNAM: The Origins of Revolution—John T. McAlister, Jr., A761

WRITINGS OF THE YOUNG MARX ON PHILOSOPHY AND SOCIETY—Loy D. Easton and Kurt H. Guddat, eds. and trans., A583

A YEAR IS EIGHT MONTHS: Czechoslovakia 1968—Journalist M A750